Also available at all good book stores

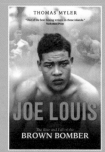

9781785315367

9781785315350

9781785315374

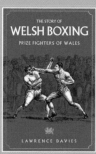

9781785315039

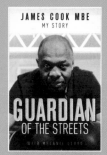

9781785314919

9781785315404

9781785315190

9781785315527

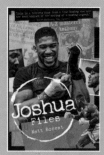

9781785313912

9781785314551

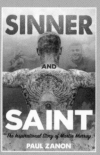

9781785313851

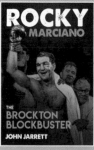

9781785313813

amazon.co.uk   W Waterstones   WHSmith

THE FINAL ROUND
WITH ABI SMITH

THE FINAL ROUND
WITH ABI SMITH

JANE COUCH
MBE

First published by Pitch Publishing, 2019

Pitch Publishing
A2 Yeoman Gate
Yeoman Way
Worthing
Sussex
BN13 3QZ
www.pitchpublishing.co.uk
info@pitchpublishing.co.uk

ISBN 978 1 78531 562 6

Typesetting and origination by Pitch Publishing
Printed and bound by TJ International, UK

Contents

Dedication: To Sara Leslie and Dinah Rose QC

Foreword

THERE aren't many people in the world who I respect and admire as much as my mate Jane. I have known her for many, many years and we became good friends in a world where she wasn't welcomed. And that's putting it nicely!

I was able to fight in the ring as soon as I made the decision I wanted to; Jane had to fight to be allowed to box. I have known a fair few boxers over the years and met a lot of fighters but Jane is both. Five times world champion? That took training, hard graft, dedication and commitment. But away from the ring she was a fighter too.

Fighting for her right to box.

Fighting for her right to box as a woman.

Fighting for her right to box as a woman in a man's world.

And I'm really proud of her. I'm proud of everything she has achieved in the boxing ring, I am proud that she stood up and took on the fight with this powerful establishment and I'm proud to call her one of my best mates.

It's down to her determination and grit and willpower that not only made her a great fighter but also made her a pioneer for women's boxing. There are several talented female boxers in Britain today that are doing us all proud. I just hope they realise they wouldn't be where they are today doing the sport they love if it wasn't for the hard work and dedication Jane put in not that long ago. She paved the way for women to be free to box in this country without fear of discrimination or abuse. No one else took on that fight and I honestly believe if it wasn't for Jane, women's boxing wouldn't be the celebrated sport it is today.

And well done for finally writing a book about it all. It's about time people see you for what you are: a history-maker, a phenomenally talented boxer, a cheeky, doggedly determined friend with a heart of gold. Someone to be celebrated.

Ricky Hatton

Prologue

My funeral

'It takes courage to live through suffering;
and it takes honesty to observe it.'

C.S. Lewis

THE sun streamed in through the kitchen window but I barely registered it as I sat there, at the table, broken.

Uncontrollable shaking had taken over my whole body. I could feel every part of me shuddering, shivering, trembling in a frenzied way and I had no power to make it stop. I looked down at my hands and saw the shaking there too, my hands which had been my power force, my fight, now just a feeble, useless extension of my body that I couldn't control.

This was as bad as it ever was and I could see it in Kim's face as she sat opposite, her hands – steady and still – clasped together on the kitchen table. Her head was tilted to one side as she scrutinised me. She had let herself in the house earlier that morning. I had listened as she called out my name but I didn't have the strength to answer. I had summoned up all my willpower to get out of bed, to make it downstairs and now I was sitting at the table, a mug of hot tea in front of me, and Kim, one of my closest friends, staring at me like I was some sort of freak show, an exhibit. The worry in her eyes gave her away. These past few weeks, everything had gotten worse, everything was an effort. I hated leaving the house, I didn't want to see anybody or talk to anybody. Leaving the house meant going out to the unknown and I would sometimes get to the front door before I would feel my breath start to quicken and in an instant I would be having a panic attack, right there in the hallway, all from the thought of opening my front door. That feeling of panic, the ringing in my ears, the cold sweat, the sense of dread ... it would be like a heavy weight pumping through me, filling every part of my body. And then the tears would start. And once that tearful feeling took over, I would be sobbing for the rest of day.

Just getting myself dressed, getting myself out of bed, was an effort. Sometimes the effort became too much and I would stay in bed all day, just lying there, just ... I don't know what I was doing really. Just breathing I suppose. Listening, breathing, surviving.

It wasn't like I could rest or sleep as I lay there. Sleeping was a joke; sleeping at night was just a distant memory to me now. I must have been able to sleep once. Of course I did; I would sleep like a baby after the training, after the fights, my body giving in to the sheer physical exhaustion. But now it was my mind controlling me and I was powerless to stop it. I would start each night thinking it would be different, thinking this was the night I would get a good rest. And then I would feel my teeth start to chatter, so I would grind them together, hard and forcefully, to make them stop, make them still. But my jaw would ache then and the tension would move down to my neck and my shoulders and I would toss and turn to try to get comfortable.

Kim told me to drink some tea. I wanted to, I really did, but I was anxious that my trembling hands would fail me. I felt a loud pulsing in my ear as I sat there, staring into the mug, head bowed because even the effort to lift it seemed too much. She started to speak but I couldn't make out what she was saying at first, the intensity of the pulsing had grown louder and I closed my eyes to try to concentrate on her voice.

'You need help ... you can't carry on like this ... look at me Jane ...

'We need to go to hospital, Jane ... let's get you help ...'

I could hear the distress in her voice as she talked; she was afraid. I was afraid. I had no answer to how I was feeling, I just knew I had never felt like this before in my life. So utterly out of control of my own body. I was an athlete, a fighter. I was strong. I was all of those things once, but I couldn't remember what they felt like now. My life had spiralled out of control since I had retired from boxing and the only life I had ever known.

Kim moved off from her chair and knelt down beside me. I had started rubbing myself all over, you know how you do when it is cold? I was rubbing my hands up and down my arms constantly, my legs jiggling up and down at the same time. I wasn't cold, it wasn't cold, it was the bloody middle of summer, but I couldn't stop. Kim made me look at her; she spoke to me. I lifted my head enough to see her lips move.

'C'mon love, let's go.'

I couldn't reply as my mouth had gone all dry, but I nodded. It was time to go. I knew she was right. I felt butterflies in my stomach as I got up. Kim held out her hand to me, to guide me out, but my hands were balled up into fists. The fighting instinct had kicked it. That fight or flight moment, the moment when you have a clarity of mind. Can I go? No. I don't need to go. I am safe here, I should just stay here. But I did go. I moved on an autopilot setting that had kicked into gear and I found myself following her out of the door and out into the unknown.

14

The hospital was only over the road so I didn't have chance to dwell on whether I should be going or not, simply that we were going and Kim was guiding me over the road. And then before I knew it we were inside and sat down together on a line of beigey-coloured plastic chairs in the waiting room. It was a warm morning and I made an effort to look around, to see how many staring eyes would be looking then looking away in embarrassment. But there couldn't have been more than a handful of people around us and no one was interested in a middle-aged woman who didn't look like she had any obvious illness or injury.

The reception area was big and Kim had guided me towards the back wall of the room, next to a table that had a few dog-eared magazines. Not that *Woman & Home* was my cup of tea, but I couldn't stop staring down at the front cover, trying to work out why it said August 2001 on the it … 2001? … that wasn't now … that was years ago wasn't it? My brain was trying to make sense of the date; was it really 2001, was there a mistake … what was the year? It was like my brain was trying to make sense of something so silly, so trivial and yet it couldn't get past it.

Kim was scribbling next to me on a clipboard; she was filling out my details. It won't be long now', I heard her say. 'The doctor won't be long.' I know people often say there is a distinctive smell to hospitals – the medicinal smell, the antiseptic smell, the smell of fear – but I don't think I could tell you what I smelt that day. My senses were switched off, they didn't care about my surroundings. I had lost all sense of attention and contemplation. I felt empty. And this emptiness, this nothingness, had come from being part of the only thing I had ever wanted: to box, to be a boxer.

All those years, I had been told what to do, where to go, when to get up. I hadn't earnt much money from it. And then you're done and the people you think care about you, the ones in the boxing world who you think have your back, who actually give a toss, say, 'OK, that's it. Fuck off now. Next!'

And then, nothing.

I heard my name being called. I was staring at a notice on the wall as I heard it. It was a poster about domestic abuse. I had read and reread the small print over and over again; it gave me something to focus on. Something else, something that wasn't to do with me.

'Physical abuse, threats, controlling behaviour ... call the Respect Phoneline ...'

'Physical abuse, threats, controlling behaviour ... call the Respect Phoneline ...'

Kim stood up first and started pulling me up next to her. I followed her towards a woman who had called my name.

Hand on my heart, I will honestly never forget the encounter I had with the doctor I saw that day. She changed my life.

She motioned over to a bed and asked me to sit on it. She drew a noisy set of curtains around the bed and stood looking at me for a while. She went through some questions – questions about my physical health, questions about my mental health … then she stopped.

She was no-nonsense, I could tell that from the astute way she was looking at me. It was like she could see right through me. Like she had seen everything I had described about feeling low, about feeling down, about feeling lost all before. And then she surprised me with a question.

'What do you see when you look at me, Jane?' she said.

And the first thing I could think of saying was, 'You've obviously done well for yourself.' It was the obvious answer. She was a doctor, she was well educated, she was earning good money.

'Do you think I have a husband and kids?' she said. 'Do you think I have a big house and a nice car?'

'Yeah,' I heard myself say. Makes sense, I thought. She probably has a holiday villa somewhere sunny too.

'Well, when I was 34 years old I had a breakdown,' she said. She was very matter-of-fact about it. She wasn't winding me up. She wasn't trying to make me feel better, she was dead serious.

'I had a nervous breakdown and I lost my kids and I lost my husband,' she said. And then she paused. She wasn't trying to elicit a response from me, she didn't want me to acknowledge what she was saying it seemed; it was like she was saying it because she was getting to a point. The conclusion of her story would be what I could now do to help myself.

'You have to do something important now Jane,' she continued. 'You have to put boxing in a coffin and bury it. Actually bury the boxing. Treat boxing like a person and have a funeral for it, grieve for it and then move on.' The way she talked to me, the way she explained things ... it was like a cloud was beginning to shift in my head. It might have sounded completely idiotic to anyone else, but she was speaking to me, and something about the way she explained it, that my life was in a state of limbo, made sense to me. *She* was explaining something about the way *I* was feeling and it made absolute perfect sense. How can that be?

She said that I was at a crossroads in my life, that I could go down one path and never escape the hold boxing had on me or I could turn around and go down the path she was suggesting. I needed to move on and the best way to do it was to bury boxing and get closure. So, as fucking crazy as it sounds, that is exactly what I decided to do. Right there on that bed, I knew I would be having a funeral later.

I walked out of hospital with a sense of purpose. I felt I had something important to do and I just had to do it now. This was my focus; I had to have a funeral for my boxing career and I had to have one today. Nothing else mattered now, I had a job to do. Kim took me back to the flat and she hung around. I knew she wanted to see if I would be

OK or if I would need her, but I was completely focused on what I had to do now. And I had to do it alone. As soon as she left, I jumped into my Jeep and drove.

I guess that has always been me: once I have an idea, once I have a mission, that's it. Determined, focused, driven, strong-minded. It's that mentality that has gotten me this far; it got me through many a fight and now I am using that same instinct to put an end to it all. I'm like a dog with a bone, I won't give up.

The church wasn't more than a ten-minute drive away and I parked up in the small, gravelly car park. I got out and realised for the first time that day how warm it was. The sun was shining; there were only a few clouds in the sky. Had it been this warm earlier? Was it this hot yesterday?

I started walking over to the graveyard. There was a small black gate that was just under waist high and I lifted the latch. Not a sound. There was no one else here, just me and the church that stood to my left and the gravestones to my left and right. There was a little stony path leading up past the gravestones and to the church and I started walking on the uneven stones. But I wasn't going to the church. I stopped and started walking on the grass now. I was walking past the headstones; some were leaning forward, like they were bowing, others stood straight upright, erect like soldiers. I started reading a few as I passed. 'Dennis Peddar, beloved husband and father ...', 'Rosemary Carter ... much loved mother ...'

Then there were some that were so old and weathered you couldn't see anything anymore. Were the people who used to visit these graves dead themselves now? Does anyone come here and lay flowers at this beaten-down old stone?

I wasn't looking for one particular spot but being near the older graves felt right. The grass was dry and prickly as I sat and crossed my legs. There was no noise at all. Nothing. Peace. I didn't have a plan or anything in my head. I hadn't been to that many funerals in my life and I wasn't particularly religious. This just felt right. It felt good. It felt controllable.

'Ashes to ashes, dust to dust,' I said out loud, to no one but myself. I probably looked like a right nutter, but I didn't care. It wasn't like the gravestones were judging me! They didn't mind. Besides, saying something out loud felt right. I had to speak the words, this had to be a proper funeral. I closed my eyes and started reciting the Lord's Prayer. I spoke each line slowly. I didn't think about anything but the words I spoke, getting a rhythm as I spoke them.

I rubbed the rosary beads that were around my neck. I had dug them out at home as soon as Kim had gone, and put them on. I don't think I had worn them properly before now. They had been a gift from a gypsy lady years ago when I would be sparring with travellers. There was a travellers' camp near where I used to train and they would come into the gym wanting to fight with anyone. They didn't care if I was a woman, they enjoyed a good spar and I certainly gave them that! After a few times of sparring with me that was it, they only ever asked for me. Every time they came back in the gym they'd ask for me by name; they weren't fussed with anyone else and I'd always be happy to get in the ring if I was around.

I smiled down at the beads as I twisted them in my fingers. This is what happens isn't it, at a funeral? The memories, the smiles of recollection, the remembering ... those fights were good fun. And the lady who had given them to me had watched me slog it out with one of the boys one evening when I had gone over to their site. She had held her hands out and quite simply said that I should have them. There was no refusing. 'Take them,' she had said, and if I ever needed anything, I was to ask Jesus for exactly what I wanted.

There is no way she could have known this day would come, that I would be sitting here now, on a warm summer's afternoon, asking Jesus to help me, asking him to help me put the boxing to bed, to forget, to bury. But that is exactly what I did.

'Please let me bury this,' I said, and closed my eyes again. 'I have had some great times and some bad times, but now I need to say goodbye. Goodbye.' I kept my eyes closed and concentrated on my breathing. In and out. Nice and steady. I didn't feel like I was losing control but

I wanted to keep myself steady, in charge. I had to do this properly.

I made myself think of some of the worst-ever moments from my career. I had to bury all the bad bits. All the hours and days and weeks of training and training and pushing myself. The time I would have happily died in the boxing ring if it meant winning my first world championship belt. Of all the hatred and venomous attacks I faced from the media and the boxing promoters when I took the British Boxing Board of Control to court because I wanted to fight legally, as a woman, in this country. Of all the lies and crap and bitterness that I faced when I won. Of all the boxing matches that I won but lost in other ways, through corruption, spite, greed. I remembered a fight I had in America. I thought I had won. I knew I had won but the judges were all American and they had given it to my opponent. It was dishonest, it was wrong and it wasn't the first or last bitter encounter I had with the world of boxing. I sat there in the changing rooms in shock.

I had been battered and I had lost a fight because of the fucked-up immoral nature of the judging. I had just lost my title and I had been ripped off by the judges; can you imagine that happening in any other sport? Could they get away with it in any other professional sport, awarding a win to the home athlete even though the opponent had clearly won. Would it happen in running? Or swimming? Of course it wouldn't! But there is so much money involved in boxing, the away fighters will always lose out when it comes to scoring because the home fighter has the judges and the crowd and everything on their side. I'm not the first person to have lost an away fight unfairly and I know I certainly won't be the last.

But I carried on. I suppose it was like staying in an abusive relationship. I stayed because all I wanted to do was box.

Breathe, breathe, breathe ... I didn't want to lose it now. Breathe, breathe ...

My mind suddenly went back in time, back to Fleetwood, to our terraced house on Albert Street and I was 11 years old, standing in the kitchen with my mum having a conversation about my future.

'I'm gonna do something big Mum, it's gonna be mental and it's gonna be big."

Is it Jane? What are you going to do love?'

'I don't know Mum, but it's gonna be big.' I smiled at the memory. I was so young and so passionate about something I was going to do, without having any idea what that something was! I thought about my younger self and then I pictured me, 26 years old now, all those years ago, eager and excited about the thought of boxing for the first time. When I had finally found something that I thought I could do and do well. 'I'm sorry,' I thought to that young version of me. 'I'm sorry you went through all that crap. I'm sorry you made choices that hurt you and I'm sorry you thought you were unworthy. You weren't ever unworthy. You did your best.'

I then said the Lord's Prayer again, I don't know why, maybe if felt right to finish on it. And then, I stood up. I bowed my head, I said, 'Goodbye', and that was it. The funeral was over.

There wasn't an immediate feeling of anything at that point, that came the next day, when I woke up and felt that there was something missing in my life. I was still the same me, I had still gone through the same horrible things – the damage still existed – but I wasn't going to let the damage control my life anymore. I had left this huge weight of fear, of anxiety, of panic; I had left it somewhere and I felt lighter. So much lighter. The weight had been lifted.

As I walked back to the Jeep I took one last look around and said 'goodbye' again. Perhaps to the other gravestones, perhaps to no one. Goodbye to the old me.

I walked back to the car calmly and with my head held up.

Ready to face the world again.

* * *

It's a funny place to start my story isn't it? Celebrating the death of my boxing career. You're probably thinking I've had one too many blows round the head, probably thinking that the fights have finally taken their toll. Ha!

I am proud of being strong enough to tell my story now because I am actually living my life now, and back then, when I was boxing, I was just surviving. I didn't set out to change history, to be the one who fought for women's boxing to be accepted.

I can't explain, even now, why I loved it. It was a mission I suppose. I wanted to box and when I found out that women couldn't do it, that was it, I had to do it. But if someone had told me the abuse I would suffer, the ridicule, the loneliness, the intimidation, the bullying, the heartache, the neglect … would I have done it? Would you? I have no feelings towards boxing now, I am detached from it and it means nothing to me.

I have given the best years of my life to boxing, I would have given my life itself for it in those early days and now I feel nothing and that sort of detachment helps you to move on. So I have, but sometimes it's important to tell a story so I am, my story.

This is the first book I have written but it isn't my first autobiography. Tex wrote the first one, straight after we won the court case. I had no interest in writing a book or being involved and however much he pestered me to contribute I refused. I just let him get on with it. But that book paints such a terrible picture of me; had I checked it or even read it, I would never have let it be published. And that's why this book is so important to me. I am ready to show people the real me, to speak honestly and frankly about my life and boxing. I'm older and wiser now and it's time I shed light on not only being 'The Fleetwood Assassin' but being 'Jane', someone who just wanted to follow her dream.

This isn't meant to be a depressing, feel-sorry-for-me tale, this is simply the truth. The truth about a world that some of you might know about. It's a story about a woman who has been battered, and has done her fair share of battering.

I hold my hands up, it's not a pretty tale and you've probably already got an idea of me being a mouthy, brassy, ballsy woman. But there is more to me than that, much, much more.

My silence about this world was, for many years, simply because I was exhausted. I was tired of fighting. And now I'm telling you about my past, it's not for you to feel sorry for me or pity me. It's so you can understand who I am, and why I am who I am. I try to go out of my way to make people feel loved and wanted because I know what it's like to not feel loved and wanted. I know what it's like to just be used and criticised. To have a dream but be torn to shreds for even thinking it.

I don't know how people are OK with themselves knowing they emotionally destroyed me, for no other reason than they didn't agree with what I wanted to be. It was a dream and I followed it through. It wasn't a childhood dream though, boxing wasn't on my radar from the word go. I didn't have a clue what I wanted to do when I was younger. And thinking back now, it's a wonder I didn't become a punk ...

Chapter One

Hey Mickey!

'Sometimes you will never know the value of
a moment until it becomes a memory.'

Dr Seuss

'WHERE have me light bulbs gone?!' Mum was furious.

Luckily, Tom and I had scarpered long before she had made the discovery that all her light bulbs had been stolen and she was shouting her head off to an empty house. I would like to say that I and my big brother felt guilty about the fact we had left Mum all alone in the dark but we'd nicked them for a good cause – one of Tom's gigs at a derelict building in a church hall the previous night. Tom was a musician in a punk rock band and we had gone out so he could play with his band, but the church hall was locked and not only did we have to break in but there were no light bulbs either. Hence us sneaking home and 'borrowing' them from the house with the aim of putting them back before Mum noticed. That didn't quite go to plan!

But the gig was worth it, even if Mum was mad as hell at us when we returned. Tom and his band were well known in the area – in Fleetwood where we lived – and I was his little roadie, his sidekick if you like. I was just accepted as one of the band I suppose. 'Oh it's just Tom's sister,' is what I usually got if anyone questioned why a nine-year-old was hanging around with a group of punk teenagers. It was so cool having a big brother in a band. I was always helping them move equipment, set up their gear – just being with them. Tom was four years older than me and was very talented. He was just starting out in the band then. He was starting to drum and write songs and our bedroom was the hub of his creativity. He'd be on the bed writing all these punk songs and listening to punk music and I'd try to join in but my heart wasn't really in it. To this day I still don't know how I didn't turn out to be a punk rocker, but I can only surmise that being surrounded by green mohicans probably put me off for life.

I didn't want to be a punk musician, that was Tom's thing. It's weird, none of my friends liked the music either and yet I was so close to Tom, I just accepted that was the world I had to be part of if I wanted to spend time with him. But I didn't want to be a punk or dress like a punk, much to Tom's annoyance.

'What's wrong with yer?!' he'd say. 'Come on Jane!'

Tom had a drum kit at home and he was constantly playing it and practising, and if he wasn't doing that punk music would be endlessly blasting out from the record player, reverberating off the walls of our terraced house. It wasn't a small house but there was no escape from the music when Tom was playing. We lived just round the corner from the market, on Albert Street in one of the larger terraces in the area. Fleetwood Market is a huge indoor market full of noise, activity and stalls that sold just about anything and everything. That isn't to say we were well-off or rich – the complete fucking opposite! – just the house was fairly large. We had no furniture in the front room as Mum would only put a fire on out the back during the winter. It made sense to her to try to just keep one room in the house warm, so the front room was left just cold and empty.

Tom was the male influence in my life growing up and he would try his best to convert me, at every opportunity, to punk. I'd wake up in the morning and I'd be treading over all these people from the punk rock world asleep on the floor and I'd have to watch out for their mohicans. They were from all the bands in the area and would come back and crash out at our house after playing in gigs all around Blackpool.

I would do my own thing with my own mates but there were only three girls on the street for me to hang out with, that was the problem. I was friends with two of them, Joanne and Janice, and then there was Gwyn, Joanne's older sister. I did spend a lot of time with Joanna and Janice and it was nice to be able to have both boys and girls to hang out with. But being with Tom would usually take precedence.

'Come on Jane, come with us, we've got a gig tonight.' And that was all I needed to hear. Tom needed me and I'd go and I'd help them move all the stuff or carry all the equipment or help them break into a hall and then we'd just have a gig there with all the punks. I was very much a tomboy but I loved playing with Janice and Joanne too and we were all very close. Although I don't think Tom appreciated me being too girly – it wasn't very cool to the punk world!

The first record I bought didn't go down too well either. It was 'Hey Mickey' by Toni Basil. Tom went completely off-his-rocker mad when he found out.

'What the fuck?!' he shouted at me, before smashing my record. 'You can't have that, what's wrong with yer Jane?!'

But even when he smashed my record I absolutely idolised Tom. Even though he would always try to convert me to being a punk!

Mum was very tolerant of Tom's music. Well, apart from when he and I stole her light bulbs for his gigs of course. Punk wasn't exactly Mum's scene either but she let him get on with it. She was very easy-going, she wouldn't fuss about the constant drumming and the bands hanging out at home and the music blaring so long as we weren't in her way. She just got used to it, I suppose. Although punk music isn't everyone's cup of tea, the fact she never told him to stop playing or practising or listening to punk is testament to the sort of woman Mum is. Strong doesn't do her justice. Resilient, tough, brave – those are the best words. Mum didn't have any parents, she grew up in an orphanage and left when she turned 18 years old, married my dad, had Tom and then I came along.

I was born on 14 August 1968 in Fleetwood, a huge fishing town that was struggling with a massive decline in the fishing industry. Life was dictated by the business of fishing – all the men went to sea to be fishermen and all the women stayed at home, working in the fishing factories and raising families. And those times were fucking hard for families with kids like me growing up in the 70s. Fishing was what put bread and butter on the table and the big dispute over fishing rights between Iceland and the UK, the Cod Wars, hit us hard. Our trawlers mainly fished the North Atlantic in search of cod, and losing those fishing grounds put extra pressure on the families trying to make a living. The men would go away for three weeks and then come back for a few days before going out to sea again. It was a way of life. We'd go down to the docks, watch them land the fish and everyone would be pleased with the haul.

The men would then go to the office and get paid, but that money had to last, it had to feed and clothe families for the three weeks the fishermen were away again. Of course, it was hard not to spend the money when you had it. The fishermen would live like kings and go on the piss for the few days they were home. Mum and her friends would go off filling the cupboards with food and kitting the kids out with clothes and shoes now they had the money to buy stuff. And then as quickly as it was spent, the men were back at sea and the money was gone. Everything went back to normal. That was the way of life, the constant cycle for most of the people growing up in our town.

I say most people; Mum never made Tom or I feel that staying and living and working in Fleetwood were our only options. Thinking back, I am amazed she had the foresight and ambition for us that she did as she could have easily, at that time, made us accept our 'fate' of the area we lived in: Tom, her eldest son, would follow in his father's footsteps and be a fisherman and as the only girl in the family I would start work in the factories, grow up and marry a fisherman and bring up my own family in the area. But such set-in-stone plans are broken when you have a strong-willed person allowing you to see that life holds more opportunities than what appeared to be on offer to us.

Mum and Dad got divorced when I was a year old and Tom was five. We didn't know what was going on; Mum never spoke badly about my dad, it was simply a case of 'they didn't get on anymore', and that's it. We never heard conversations about important stuff. Adults never discussed 'adult' stuff when we were around so we never really knew how bad things were or what was happening.

If Mum's friends came round that was it: 'Right kids, go upstairs or go in the other room or go out and play. Go on, out you go!' There was an element of protecting us from their conversations; they didn't want us to hear what they were saying. If you talk in front of kids you expose them to an adult world so we never knew the ins and outs of stuff. We knew what we needed to know and that was all. She was very protective was Mum, she still is. Even now, she's terrible.

'What you had for your tea?' she demanded, when she rang me the other day.

'What?'

'Have you had your tea?' she repeated. She had her not-to-be-messed-around voice on.

I sighed. 'Mum I'm 50 years old,' I said, 'I …'

'You still got to eat!' she went on.

She's the same with my brother, too. She'll tell him off for looking tired and working too hard. If I go away travelling now she's on edge until I get back. I'll have to ring her when I'm away so she knows I'm OK. Or if I call her when I'm out somewhere in the evening she's not happy until I am home.

'Get yourself in now love, get yourself in,' she'll often say, like she did when I was a kid out playing with the boys. Bless her. I think she thinks I'm out in a war zone or something. But we are very close and I have enormous respect for her and the way she never made me or Tom feel we were simply just destined for a life in Fleetwood.

With Mum and Dad divorcing at my young age, I never knew life to be any different. Home was me, Mum and Tom. We'd see Dad on a Sunday, probably not as regularly as we should have, and would just visit him and his new family. It was just normal, there was no bad feeling. Tom and I kept our distance a bit, Dad had his new life and Mum had met a fisherman not long after they divorced called Lenny Smith and remarried. Lenny was in our life probably more than my dad, but he would go to sea for weeks at a time, so in lots of ways it was just Mum raising us by herself.

And Mum was very clever. She worked in the offices at the factories where they made the boxes and nets for the fishermen. They used to fix the nets in those factories, but Mum, who was bright and had done well at school, worked instead in the office part of the factory. She met a lady there called Madeline and when Mum turned 18 and left the orphanage, she went to live with Madeline and her family. Tom and I called her Auntie Mad and she and her husband Bill, who we called Uncle Bill, and their kids John, Annabelle, Angela and Tony became like family.

When Mum first met Dad, when she worked in the offices, they were happy. I know she said the pressure of where they lived, where there was little work, little money and little prospect, took its toll on their relationship. Then she had Tom and me, money was tight and the fishing started to decline … it would put a strain on anyone, on any relationship. And I admire them for divorcing. It wasn't very common back then but there was never any bad blood, never any blame. You didn't air your laundry in public, you just got on with it. You dealt with whatever life dealt you and you didn't complain.

* * *

We'd quite often go down to the docks and watch the fishing boats leave or land. Mum was always dropping into conversations some of the negative things about being a fisherman, the hard times, the troubles, the upheaval of leaving your family.

'Oh you don't want to go to sea do yer, Tom? What would anyone want to go to sea for?' she'd say. It was her subtle way of saying, 'there is a future beyond this fishing town, beyond being a trawlerman.'

Mum knew how hard it was earning money and raising a family in these conditions, she was simply getting us to think of a future outside of Fleetwood.

Tom had no desire to be a fisherman, his dream was music and his band, a future away from Fleetwood and she had givien her blessing to this future. It was brave, to put him off that life, as in those days that's all there was for the men to do, that was their life, grow up and be a fisherman. The men would go to sea and the women would work in the sea houses or factories and raise families.

'I don't want you to go to sea Tom but if you want to go, go,' she said. And you know what? He did go a few times. It's called 'pleasuring' and he went out for three weeks to be a helper on the boat, and when he landed he was given some money. But it didn't suit him; he tried it, but it wasn't his future. Maybe he felt a sense of duty to try it, perhaps a deep-rooted idea that he had no choice but to try it, no matter what Mum said, but it just wasn't him. He was in love with his music.

I had no interest in anything as a child, no hobbies, no pursuits, no real passions. Mum didn't want my future to be here as a fisherman's wife. The problem is, when you are a kid, you don't realise all the things your parents do for you, in a subtle way, that shapes who you are. I don't think, even when I was boxing, I realised what a strong, supporting influence Mum was. At no point was there any expectation of us staying in Fleetwood and living the life that was mapped out for people of my generation. She was ahead of her time in that respect: here was a woman who had never left Fleetwood, had spent her whole life in the same place, struggling to put food on the table and yet she was always looking to inspire us to be different.

'What do you want to do Jane love?' she'd ask me, and I'd go, 'I don't know Mum, I'm no good at school but I'm gonna do something and it's gonna be big.'

'Is it Jane? What? What are you going to do love?'

'I don't know Mum, but it's going to be big …'

When I look back now at how she must have managed, it must have been so hard to raise a family practically as a single parent and keep a home running on and us fed on hardly any wage. And yet she just got on with it. It was matter of fact – stop moaning, get on with it and keep going. That was her attitude to life. And if I'm looking for remarkable role models or resilience personified I would need to look no further than my Mum. She had no parents and me and Tom were her world, and even though she couldn't give us much in terms of material possessions, she gave us a future.

Lenny lived at home with us when he wasn't at sea, and when he was home we had money. But times were pretty tough when he was away and we had to scrape by. So although it was hard in that sense, my childhood was by no means desolate. We knew the value of friendship and family, and Tom and I used to try to help bring money in, in our own childish ways. That's when we had the most laughs, trying to make money for Mum, that's how you learnt your life skills. And me and Tom, we were thick as thieves. And Bozzy, of course. He was our best friend and lived next door to us. His real name was Christopher

Boswell and when his dad or his brother were in from the sea, they'd look after us, and then when Lenny was home we'd look after Bozzy. That is how it was, everyone was coping with the same situation and when one fisherman went to sea, another one was probably just landing so the families would all help each other out.

It meant you could just about survive. The fishermen would be landing at different times so you could borrow a fiver from someone until your dad or brother or whoever got back from sea and then you'd pay it back. And Mum would help out other women if Lenny was home; she'd always give them a few quid until their husbands landed. It was the way of life, it was about surviving and making the most of what you had. It was real community spirit, there wasn't any question of not helping, it just happened. And if Lenny was home from sea, chances are Mum would want to spend time with him and go out for the three days and nights in the pub around the corner. She'd never lock the front door, you didn't need to, everyone knew everyone else and quite often the neighbours would pop in and check on me and Tom. Or we'd go round to Bozzy's house and have tea with them or the three of us would go and knock on the window of the Legion where Mum and Lenny were and she'd come out with some money and tell us to go to the chippy for our tea.

Then when Bozzy's dad was back from sea, he'd be round our house, Mum would feed him without question.

I can still see him, clear as day, walking through the front door into the kitchen, and Mum would say, 'Dad back Bozzy love?'

'Yeah, Mum's in the Legion with him,'

'Sit yerself down then, have some tea.'

There was no asking or permission, it was just a way of life. You just got on with it and it was the norm. You didn't make an appointment to pop round, you just walked in and everyone treated you like you were at home. Of course Bozzy's mum Claire wanted to spend time with his dad, Big John; they hadn't seen each other, so yes, Bozzy's with us. And Claire never minded me and Tom round their house cos Lenny was back and Mum was out with him. We were in and out of each other's houses like we had two homes, it was just like having extended family next door. Claire, Big John and Bozzy's brother, John, would always make us feel welcome. I loved sleeping over with Claire when Big John was at sea, and Tom and I spent a lot of time just at their house, it was just the norm. You never felt like you were just an isolated family, you were part of something bigger, part of other families, and Tom and I thought of Bozzy and John as brothers.

John became a deckhand on a fishing boat like his dad, and although he was a little bit older than us he was always looking out for me. He took me to the Fleetwood carnival one year. It is a big annual event and everyone gets dressed up in these weird and wonderful costumes.

Mum didn't have enough money to get me a costume and I remember sitting on the corner of Albert Street, crying my eyes out. I was only 9 years old and was desperate to get dressed up and be part of it. John found me and saw how upset I was and told me not to worry, I would go to the ball, or in this case, carnival. We had two hours before it began so there was time to get dressed up and he gave me his big black boots to wear, which were absolutely massive for my little feet, and wrapped me up in a black bin liner. He painted my face black and walked me over to the carnival and entered me as the 'binman'. I ended up winning first prize! It was the best moment ever. I had been so upset thinking I wasn't even going to be entered and now I had a rosette with first on it. I was properly chuffed with that.

There was a bloke called George Roberts who lived on our street; he was the nicest kid in the world and he'd always be round our house, happy to babysit if Lenny had docked and Mum wanted to go out. His mum, Jessie, knew my mum, although they weren't friends, and there were several occasions when I'd come home and walk into the kitchen and there would be George, sitting at the table while Mum was putting his hair in rollers.

'What you doing to George's hair, Mum?' I asked once. I must have been about six years old.

'He just wants his hair done, leave 'im alone!' she'd reply, like it was the most natural thing in the world to put his hair in curlers. 'Go on with yer, mind your own business!' and that was that.

George had the most horrific upbringing, there isn't any other way to describe it. His dad, Phillip, was a trawlerman, an alcoholic and a bully of a man who beat and tried to rape George when he was a child. He was the oldest of eight children and Jessie, who was also an alcoholic, had tried to kill herself several times. How anyone deals with that and doesn't become bitter and twisted and full of hate I just don't know, but George was the sweetest, kindest soul and probably sought some sort of solace in our home, in our kitchen and with Mum doing his hair.

It was probably only a few years later that he left Albert Street, moved to Manchester and set up a drag club. And in 1979 BBC2 filmed a documentary on him as he became the first transgender person to have his transition documented on mainstream TV. I remember Mum, Tom and I all crowded around the telly to watch the show.

'Where's George gone?' I said to Mum as we watched the TV. And then, 'Is that George?! Why is he turning into a woman?!'

I couldn't get my head round what I was watching, I was having flashbacks of him sitting in curlers in our kitchen and now I was watching telly and there was our babysitter having surgery to turn him into a woman, Julia Grant.

There was so much backlash from people at that time, the stereotypical attitudes of people being that this was unnatural and wrong. And yet, knowing George and knowing that this was obviously something he wanted to do, in my 11-year-old mind, that's all that mattered. And maybe it opened our eyes to the world a bit more; maybe a deep-rooted sense of tolerance was instilled in us those times when George was around having his hair done and when we saw him on TV becoming Julia. If he was happy, what did it matter?

There was always an overwhelming sense of community to our upbringing. Mum's best friend, Jackie, would go to the clothes shop round the corner for us sometimes and just nick loads of stuff then bring it to our house. Bold as brass she was. 'I got all these off the rails at Mickey's', she'd say to Mum. 'Give 'em to kids.' And that was that, we'd be trying all these clothes on she'd just robbed. It was all about survival.

So growing up in a northern sea town, no it wasn't that bad. There were good bits to remember as well as the bad. We didn't have much money but we lived and we got by. And the good bits were definitely Tom and Bozzy, they were my absolute world. When Lenny was away fishing, it was like a challenge for us – how would we get money for coal for the fire or pennies for the TV – and I have to say, we were pretty creative. There was one Guy Fawkes night when we dressed up Bozzy as a 'Guy' and we'd go and sit outside pubs. When the fishermen stumbled out we'd be waiting, looking suitably pleading, with Bozzy in between us calling out, 'Penny for the Guy? Penny for the Guy?'

And if they had just got back from their trips away we'd be in luck and they'd be happy to give us loads of change. The drunker they were the more generous they'd be and we'd run home with pockets full of change for Mum.

At Christmas, the three of us would go round and sing carols up and down the street, trying to earn a few quid. It was so much fun. I'm pretty sure this was the only time Tom would have anything to do with music that wasn't punk rock! Other than that, we'd simply spend the days wandering up and down Albert Street asking if people needed any odd jobs doing. Sometimes we'd be in luck and we'd clean cars or clear the garden for some money and because the neighbours all knew the three of us, they'd all try to help if they could and give us little jobs. We were like the three musketeers. And the musketeers always help others don't they? We used to use my doll's pram to collect coal for the elderly residents in the street. Mrs Bertwhistle always got the most coal because she would give us 20 pence!

But even the musketeers got into fights didn't they? Thing is, life was pretty tough, you learnt how to shout – mouthing off was the norm – and you learnt how to look after yourself.

Our road was fairly near a council estate and we'd quite often be fighting with kids from over there. If we had a bommy (bonfire), they would sneak over and steal the wood in the middle of the night so then we'd go round and steal it back. We'd normally get caught stealing it back so you had to learn how to stick up for yourself, you had to learn, very early on, how to fight.

'Just fucking punch 'em in the face, Jane', Tom would shout, 'then leg it!' and I'd stand there, fists raised, ready to take them on, being a distraction while he and Bozzy nicked back the wood.

'Alright then!' I'd shout, ready for action. Probably sounding braver than I felt. But I wasn't scared. I wasn't scared one fucking bit. It was bloody brilliant, I was with Tom and Bozzy and all the boys and I'd just copy what they'd do, swing my arms and kick out. I had no fear. If I came unstuck it didn't' matter, I'd have the boys helping me wouldn't I? The three musketeers.

I can only fight because of my upbringing with the boys. There was a patch of grass opposite the house and if we had arguments we'd then be like, 'Right! Let's have it!' And Tom would shout, 'Jane against Bozzy, I'll go against …' and so on and so on.

So we'd all just be fighting all the time, it's how I learnt to fight and it was just the norm. The scraps Tom, Bozzy and I would get into, it's ridiculous. We'd fight all the time us three, that's how we passed the time. There were no computer games or Game Boys or Youtube, we'd be sitting there in the front room of Bozzy's house and then we'd just start fighting. It was something to do. Either I'd be on Tom's back trying to bring him down or Bozzy would pin me down and tickle me, tickle my feet and just try to strangle me. But then Mum would come in and batter the pair of them and shout at them both for fighting with me and she'd throw them out.

I'd then get really upset and plead with her, 'No Mum, I want to go with Bozzy and Tom.' I was so upset, I wanted to be with them!

And Mum would be incredulous. 'But they've just battered yer Jane!'

'I know but ...'

It was like our playing. It was how we passed the time. I had lots of friends, all the kids on Albert Street knew each other and got on. We'd always be playing or fighting or I'd jump on Tom's back and my mate Joanna would jump on Bozzy's back and they'd be our horses and we'd be the soldiers. So there was a bit of innocence to it, but it was also about learning skills that you would need as you got older, living where we did.

Did I go to school much? Not really. You didn't have to go to school in those days. OK, you did, I know that, but school wasn't really a big part of my life. We'd all set off for school in the morning but there were plenty of times we didn't actually get there. Nobody ever really said much so we'd just carry on doing that, going on some days, most days not. School was hard and I struggled. I wasn't academically gifted and I struggled to concentrate and struggled to focus on what I was told to do. Honestly, I just couldn't be bothered to learn so I never really put in a lot of effort. Some days I went just to pass the time but then I'd get into trouble and think why'd I bother? I got into plenty of fights at school but mostly because I was always sticking up for people. There was a girl called Caroline who was mixed race and this made her a massive target for bullies because there weren't any black people in those days in Fleetwood. It was quite a racist place back then, and although her mum was white, her dad was black and she used to get picked on really badly by other kids at school. So I'd fight on her behalf, I'd stick up for her and another girl called Marie who would get picked on. So the fights were nothing to do with me really, but I was so angry that these girls were being bullied, I would get stuck right in!

'Fuck off, leave 'em alone!' I'd shout, almost as a threat that if the bullies didn't back off they'd have me to deal with. I would fight for the ones that didn't fight back, the different kids who were just trying to fit in and didn't have the balls, like I did, to stand up to bullies. I'm not saying that justifies all my school scraps, but in a sense to me, all I was doing was helping those kids who didn't have the skills I did. The skills I had learnt from Tom and Bozzy.

There is one afternoon I remember with the boys very well. We were in the sitting room at Bozzy's house, just listening to punk rock and chatting. It wasn't an unusual occurrence, we'd spend hours together like this, just chatting away. Bozzy's home was our second home, Bozzy's mum Claire always had a pan of boiled eggs on the stove and other treats for us, they were just like our extended family next door. But this afternoon, this was the first time I knew things were going to change. I had the feeling Tom was getting ready to tell us something.

'I'm gonna be a big rock star,' Tom said. 'It's gonna happen. I'll be a famous drummer in a big band and we'll be on *Top of the Pops*.' That was his ambition, that was the goal for Tom.

'What about you Boz? What's your dream?' Tom asked.

'Own me own fishing boat,' Bozzy said, without hesitation.

And then it was my turn, and I didn't know what to say. I had these two boys who I thought the world of and I wanted to explain that I had a dream, only I didn't have one.

'I don't know what I'm going to do but it's going to be massive,' I said. Like I had said to Mum before. It's like I believed that something was possible, there was something I was destined to do but I had no idea what it was. I think having a brother who dreamed such big dreams about music, stardom and fame had a massive influence. There was a big future out there for him, why not me? I just didn't know what it was yet.

In the end, our dreams discussed in Bozzy's small living room that afternoon did come true. Tom left Fleetwood at 15 years old and went to America with his band. He wasn't going to let anyone stand in the way of his dreams and he left our small fishing town for the bright lights, money and opportunity of America. As it turned out, Tom and his band, One Way System, went on to be the first signing for Cherry Red's Anagram Records and he played with the punk rock band UK Subs for two years. One of his songs with One Way System was called 'Give Us a Future' and he has been voted one of the top-30 best punk drummers of all time. So being a Fleetwood fisherman was never on the cards for Tom. He was the first famous 'Couch'. But not the last.

And Bozzy? Bozzy did become a deckhand on a fishing boat but several years later he died at sea. He went out on his boat one day and went overboard, lost at sea. I got the phone call when I was in America, preparing for one of my boxing matches. Tom rang me, totally out of the blue, and he just said, 'Bozzy's dead'. Just like that. And it took a while to process what I'd heard and I think I went into a state of shock. I hadn't seen Bozzy for years but as soon as Tom rang and told me the news, all those childhood memories came flooding back. He was like another brother, he was the third musketeer and I couldn't understand why he was gone. I honestly don't know how I was in the right frame of mind to fight that night. I was devastated and I just wanted to sit back and take it all in, but I wasn't allowed. People around me then didn't have a clue who Bozzy was, they didn't give a shit. They just wanted me to box – I had a job to do and there was no time to grieve or dwell or get upset. But by God I'll never forget him. Me, Boz and Tom … those times being with them were so special. I was heartbroken. I was heartbroken for that childhood friend who died living a life that was ultimately his dream.

Chapter Two

Police, punch-ups and prison

'Hard times are often a blessing in disguise.
Your past was never a mistake if you
learned from it.'

Manisha Shrestha Bundela

FIGHTING and brawling on the streets meant that it wasn't long before I wasn't spending much time at school. I didn't want to go, I hated it there and it didn't bother me in the slightest when I was expelled. I didn't need school, I just wanted to follow my brother out into the world and discover for myself a life outside of Fleetwood. I missed Tom terribly when he left for America. He was only 15 years old, which is bloody young whichever way you look at it, but being in a band was his vision and he was unstoppable.

But his leaving, well, it was unheard of in Fleetwood. Leaving for America to be in a punk rock band? He was like a god! He was my hero and I was his greatest champion. He rang us from America but because we didn't have a phone at home we'd have to go to the docks and use a phone in one of the offices there. We had a friend called Bunny Walker who would let us use his and we'd get to speak to Tom all the way from bloody America. It blew my ten-year-old mind.

'I've seen a skyscraper,' he'd say.

'Wow, what's it like? Tell me!' I'd ask, and then he'd go on about all the other cool stuff he'd seen and that the band were playing here and then there and the single was going to be released … and it was just overwhelming.

'Brilliant, Tom, that's brilliant. There is fuck all going on here!' Mum and I would say. 'Come home and save us!' But he never did.

I was so happy for him. He had a dream and he followed it and he was doing what he loved. He'd moved away and was making a new life for himself and was seeing all these famous people and I was happy for him. And jealous.

'I want to do that,' I'd say to Mum.

'But Jane, love, you don't play an instrument,' was Mum's answer.

I missed him terribly. It's hard to explain really. I was pleased for him yet so sad because selfishly I wanted him to be with me. I needed him but I didn't realise how much until he'd gone. He was a bit of a hero.

My teenage years were pretty fucked up. I was getting into fights, had been expelled, and yet, in the back of my mind, I was thinking … I'm better than this, why am I doing it? And the answer was simply because it was what it was. I'm not making excuses, that was just the life. There were so many newspaper reports about me when I became famous. But Fleetwood did teach me some things. The school of life I think you call it now, but back then it was just about getting on and making the best of the crap you had. My first boyfriend was Dave Smith and his mum and dad owned the Kings Arms pub. This was one of the biggest pubs in Fleetwood, an impressive, red-brick building that stood on the corner of Lord Street and was the place that most fishermen went when they landed. I was still relatively young, about 14 years old, when I started working there behind the bar. I'm not sure you'd be able to get bar work that young these days that's for sure, but Dave's mum and dad, Kath and Alan, taught me everything there was to know about pub work. They took me on, showed me and taught me the ways of the pub. And they didn't care – I was young, I was eager and I was not afraid of being surrounded by loud, fighting drunks so I was useful to them too. I wasn't just serving pints, they taught me the whole pub trade – cashing up, changing barrels, serving ... I could run a pub on my own from what they taught me in those days. They were big characters, Kath and Alan. They were very well-known, not-to-be-messed with landlords in Fleetwood and I learnt not just about the pub game but their strength of character rubbed off on me too. I was young and impressionable and, having only really had Bozzy and Tom to hang around with, I was suddenly exposed to an adult world of toughness and fighting.

It wasn't isolated incidents, the fights, the scraps, the trouble. In those days, it was just what it was. You expected trouble in Fleetwood, it just had that name. Everyone knew it, the people who lived their knew it, the fishermen ... times were bloody hard for a lot of people and the anger and the fear and the pressure of money was bubbling very close to the surface all the time. It didn't take much for someone to snap. The fishermen brawls were most common and predictable I suppose. Every time the Irish fishermen landed in town they would want a good fight. And then there were the Icelandic fishermen – we'd call them 'Scrobs' – and when they landed the locals would get all defensive and be after any excuse for a fight too.

'You looking at my woman, Scrob? What you lookin' at?!' And then it would begin. I remember Lenny once eye-balling this Scrob once for looking at Mum – or he thought he was looking at Mum. It was a matter of principle I guess. Normally the Scrobs would land and just be looking for a bit of fun. If all the local fisherman were away they would get that with the women who didn't mind cheating on their husbands. These sort of fights, the fishermen brawling, this was just normal to us. We'd be walking down the street into town and there would be a pair of them going for it on the other side of the road or outside of the pubs you passed. You just sort of stepped over them or walked around.

'Cross over the road,' Mum would say, 'take no notice!'

Kath was a very hard-working woman who was as hard as fuck, so was her old man. She didn't stand for any trouble and she commanded a sort of respect from all the punters who came in. If you made trouble, you were out. And when you were running a pub full of fishermen, you had to be a certain kind of person! But the pub was also a community hub too; the fishermen would come back, families would be reunited briefly, have money to spend and want to have a good night out. Kath and Alan would be drinking and working and drinking some more with them, like most good landlords do I suppose. And Dave and I enjoyed being there with them.

Most nights we'd be in the pub, keeping out of the way upstairs. You could always hear all the commotion that would be happening downstairs though, the fishermen shouting and fighting and then Kath and Alan shouting and throwing them out. It was normal background noise to me and Dave, who would just be sitting upstairs playing Elvis records. Some nights we'd be summoned to lend a hand – Kath would suddenly shout upstairs, 'Bring a bag of 50s down Jane!' rr 'Bring me a bag of 1s downs. Hurry up love!'

She was hard as nails that woman. But was she tough before she ran a pub or did running that pub make her tough? You certainly didn't ever want to cross her. I suppose I was a little bit in awe back then; if anyone gave her any shit, well, that was it, they were out. She had so much power. In the mornings, Kath and Alan would stay in bed and Dave and I would go downstairs first thing and start clearing up, wiping down, cleaning all the pump lines. There was a bookmakers next door too, and Dave showed me how to bet. He took me in and explained all about placing a bet and what to look for. I learnt a lot from this family!

And, ironically, it was outside the Kings Arms when I got arrested for the first time. It was hard, the teenage years were problem times, not just for me, everyone seemed to be finding it tough. No one quite knew where to fit in after leaving school, some of us had started work and were trying to figure out what to do with our lives. Everyone was, well, wild. I'd be out in Fleetwood most weekends, going out getting into fights, going to prison. It was the norm, that is what my teenage years consisted of, going out, going to the park, drinking with boys, fighting.

There was a memorial park not far from home and we would quite often go in there, hang around by the tennis courts and have a drink. Mates would gather there, we'd see who'd turn up and then we might just wander home, wander round the streets for a bit or go off to the sea cadets disco. Although most times, when we got to the disco, everyone just ended up fighting!

And then the next night we'd all meet up again and talk about what a cracking night we'd had and everyone would want to know who battled who … it was just one big game. Nothing mattered to us, getting in scraps was just the norm. Getting injured? Sure, of course you did!

I'd get black eyes and busted lips but it wasn't anything I wasn't used to. I had fought for years with Bozzy and Tom so I didn't mind, it wasn't anything I hadn't felt before. Getting a black eye sounds impressive but, really, the shock of it is over pretty quick and you don't really feel much. And then it swells up like a good 'un so there was no disguising what you'd been up to.

When I was 15 years old, life changed a bit for me – I moved to London with Tom. He'd come back from America with his band to concentrate on his music here and moved in with his girlfriend Julie – they had a little place in Clapham.

'Wanna come for the weekend?' he said to me.

'Alright then!' I said, and that was that. Goodbye Fleetwood! I got the bus to London, it took about eight long, uncomfortable hours, but I was out of Fleetwood and I was going to be with Tom so it was worth it. Tom said he had a flat in Clapham but it was more of a bedsit, there was just one room with a little kitchen and a bed, so when I turned up it was a bit of a squeeze! Three of us sleeping in one little room wasn't ideal, but they looked after me, they never made me feel like I wasn't welcome. I ended up staying longer than the weekend, I think I stayed on and off for about seven years in the end!

I got a job in a hotel and then left that and moved to a pub in Clapham Common – the Railway Tavern. Then I got another job in another pub, and another. I was constantly chopping and changing, moving around different jobs, but I was always working. I was independent, it was just how it was. I'd seen Mum doing the same, when there was no electric and she didn't have 10p to put in the meter, there was that incentive to earn money. Earn money just to watch telly! I wasn't afraid of hard work and I loved working in the pubs. I had had good training of course, working in the Kings Arms and learning from Kath and Alan was all the guidance I needed, and I ended up pretty much running several of the pubs I worked in in London. I enjoyed that, it was fun, there were always new people to chat to, new people to meet, new things to learn. I didn't ever just want to sit around at Tom's flat by myself doing nothing, that wasn't me, I'd be working day and night and having a right laugh.

And I would go back to Fleetwood and see my mates and stay with Mum on occasions. It was probably this time that I was getting into trouble with the police.

Remember I said the first time I got nicked was outside the Kings Arms? That was a massive fight outside the pub and when the cops turned up I ended up jumping through one of the windows of the jewellery shop opposite. They dragged me out and I was sent to prison. I've been arrested so many times it's hard to remember exactly what for and when ... that sounds fucking bad doesn't it?! I can't hide from the truth, from the past. It's what happened but I'm not proud of it. I was probably in and out of prison every other week for a period. There was a fight or there was this or that. I got a car when I was 16 years old but I didn't have any tax or insurance, so I was always getting stopped by the police when I went out. It was a bloody nightmare! If I went out with my mates I'd drop them all off home after a night out and then get nicked on my way home. Thinking about it now, I'm not sure I had a licence either, I just drove! I was coming and going between London and Fleetwood, staying with Tom then coming back, and between those two places I probably had quite a record sheet going.

I wasn't scared of the police, I had no fear whatsoever in those days – of anyone or anything. Be that a cocky youngster talking or a person who just simply wasn't afraid and knew how to look after herself. I was battered many times by different coppers when I was nicked but that's how it was back then. They'd arrest you and your mates, knock you around a bit so you knew who was boss, leave you in a cell for a bit then take you home. Mum was fucking furious whenever I was brought home by the cops, she would go absolutely mental. Of course, she'd stick up for me if they said anything bad against me, but once they had gone she'd take off her Scholl sandals, those heavy wooden ones, and batter me with one for good measure. Then she'd try to say I had to stay in and wasn't to go out but that would only last a couple of hours. I'd probably get under her feet too much and I'd be sent back out!

Being continually in trouble with the police meant that I had a supervision order and I was on probation, but the seriousness of that never really hit home. I'd quite often miss meetings that I was meant to attend, and the upshot was after one too many forgotten about probation checks I had to appear in court. And again, whether this became the norm for me I'm not sure, but I ended up getting a court summons and not particularly caring. But there was only a certain number of times this would happen before the judge decided that enough was enough, and due to my lack of respect and appearance at court I was now facing serious jail time. I ended up getting three months once for flouting the rules and missing probation. I openly admit that I just couldn't be bothered. I'd receive the letters, I'd be told what I needed to do but I just couldn't give a fuck so it wasn't anyone else's fault but mine.

And you know what? Serving time at Her Majesty's pleasure turned out to be brilliant fun. I was sentenced, together with my friend Carol, for three months and we ended up serving just six weeks. So even if it was crap it wasn't like I had to be there for long! Carol and I ruled that prison from the very first moment we got there to the time we left. It was like a fucking holiday camp to us and at no point did we ever think, 'Shit, we're in prison ... we need to sort ourselves out as we don't want to come back here ever again.' It just wasn't like that at all for me, I think I probably thought it was a rite of passage. I've served some time, so fucking what?

I was about 21 years old and Carol was only 19 when we were incarcerated, and she was pregnant. We were so young, didn't give a shit about anyone and we had such a laugh. She didn't want anyone to know she was pregnant, and she begged me not to say anything even though I knew she'd get extra care and stuff. She was adamant no one was to know.

'Don't you fucking tell them Jane, don't say aught,' she'd say. And of course I was her best mate so I kept quiet. It wasn't my place to tell anyone if she didn't want to. We had been sent to Drake Hall Prison near Stoke-on-Trent. It has since become a closed women's prison, but back then it was all fairly relaxed and you could leave your cells during the day and wander around.

Carol and I made an impression on the inmates pretty much as soon as we arrived. There were a couple of ladies who didn't like the look of us – a young pair who didn't give a fuck. We pretty much radiated cockiness when we walked in, almost taunting others to try, to just try to pick a fight with us. The ladies who had the problem, the ones that had been in prison for some years, acted like they owned the place, like it was their prison and things were done their way. Well, that was all well and good for them I suppose but where did that leave us? Sometimes you have to confront these sort of characters head on, so Carol and I did, we gave them a bit of a battering and moved on.

We didn't hold grudges or make trouble, we dealt with what we needed to and that was it. Things soon found a level playing field and there was no more trouble. Mind you, anyone who didn't like us could just fuck off!

And I'd love to say it was tough and I never wanted to see the inside of a prison ever again, but I was sharing a cell with my best mate, we were getting fed and watered three times a day – what wasn't to like? OK, it was still prison and that wasn't great, but we were there for six weeks and, the way I looked at it, it could have been worse.

The best thing about it was our allotted 'job' whilst we were inmates, which was to work in the garden. It was a lot better than being stuck in the hot kitchen so we were able to get out in the fresh air and mess around. I can't say a lot of gardening actually went on but I'm sure we did a bit!

The garden was right by the road so Carol sussed out pretty quickly that she could get her Dad to chuck a bag of stuff over the wall to us. It was the perfect situation. He used to bring stuff like cigarettes, phone cards, alcohol, chocolate and sweets, shove it all into a holdall, and when we were in the garden he'd chuck it over. It was ideal and we got pretty good at giving him the signal when it was all clear. Then we'd take it all back to our little prison cell and work out what to sell it for. The fags and the phonecards would be the best earners and we would absolutely rip the piss out of selling it, making a good cut. For example, a £10 phonecard we'd sell for £25 and a packet of 20 fags we'd sell for a tenner – which was a lot of money back then!

There was one hairy moment when I was in the garden and Carol's dad chucked a bag over and I was spotted and chased back to my cell. Carol was asleep in her bunk so when I flew in, trying not to draw attention to myself, I just chucked the bag at her, in bed, and I climbed up into my bunk, pretending to be asleep. When the guards came in I pretended to be all sleepy like I had been woken up and poor old Carol, she had no idea what was going on, she had a bag to try to hide and she had just woken up!

'You bastard!' she said to me when they had gone, 'fucking bastard.' And I couldn't help but laugh as it was bloody funny as the look on her face was priceless! And we still had the bag full of stuff so she wasn't mad at me for long.

Of course, however much Carol and I treated it as a bit of a joke, it was still prison and there were some dodgy characters in there. I was in the kitchen once, talking away to quite a nice lady – or so I thought.

'What the fuck you talking to her for?!' fumed Carol when she walked in.

'Whatcha mean?'

'Don't talk to her Jane, she's fucking killed her baby,'

Silence. 'Well … you don't know the story Carol, she's alright she is.'

'It doesn't matter, no one's allowed to talk to her.'

And that was that. I can't remember her name, I just remember feeling sorry for the woman at the time and that she was quite nice. And Carol is dead now so I can't ask her who it was. When we left prison we slowly sort of drifted apart, our lives went in different directions. We were such good mates in those days but life just took us on different paths. I ended up leaving Fleetwood not long after our stint in prison but Carol went back, had her baby, and never left.

This picture I'm painting, this view of Fleetwood, growing up there, is just how I remember it. I'm not saying it to shock or impress or make you feel sorry for my upbringing. It is just memories, it was what it was. I had a loving mum and brother and mates, and at no point did I feel I was getting a raw deal or hated any of it. I guess it's important for me to explain my childhood but that's as far as it goes. Of course, life would have been different if I'd grown up somewhere else, that's true for anyone. But it turned out that my Fleetwood childhood did help me. A lot of what was reported, about me growing up, getting into fights, always making trouble and always getting into trouble, well, I guess it wasn't far from the truth. But not because I sought it and not because I wanted it, it was just what life was growing up. And I am sure there are thousands of people who grew up in fishing towns in the 1970s who would argue that life wasn't like that for them. And great, I'm pleased for you, I really am. But that is how it was for me and I had a wonderful childhood, I didn't not feel loved, not once, and I had the best inspiration right in front of me – Tom. He could dream of being a famous punk rocker, so there must be something out there for me …

It wasn't long after prison that I decided I'd had enough of London and moved back to Fleetwood permanently. I had enjoyed my time in the big smoke but I think I was living under a bit of an illusion to begin with. I was drawn to getting out of Fleetwood, to leave and see the bright lights of London; it was such a drive for me, so when Tom called and told me he was staying in the capital … well, I didn't need asking twice. And it was great for a while, I earnt some money, I went out partying, I got good tips from punters and I spent time with Tom. I had my hand forced a little bit. Lenny had died and I guess I felt bad for Mum so when I moved back to Fleetwood, although I was happy to go, it was also pretty good timing. Lenny had lost his job as a fisherman and he couldn't find himself any other work and started drinking heavily. He spent most of the time getting pissed and eventually it was the death of him.

Mum met a new man a few years later, Bunny Walker, who was a lovely fella and lived in the flats nearby. He was the bloke who had let us use his phone when Tom first moved to America so they had known each other for a while and, although they didn't live together, he'd take her out and would look after her. I'm sad to say he ended up dying too, so she's currently on her own. Mind you, she's 81 years old and there is no sign of her slowing down.

'I've just been up Blackpool Jane, got a bit of shopping done,'

'Mother, you're 81! Whatcha need to go to Blackpool for?!'

'Stop your grumbling,' she said. 'What you eaten today? Have you had your tea yet?' I couldn't argue with her if I tried. I think these little shopping trips for her now are her slice of luxury. Going out to buy something. Having money in your purse to spend on yourself was an extravagance she just didn't have when I was younger, so I don't blame her.

Moving back to Fleetwood in my mid-20s and living with Mum was, in fact, a turning point in my life. And there was something about the place I missed if I'm honest; I missed the people. Everyone knew everyone and looked out for each other. You don't get that sense of community in London, it doesn't happen. OK, forget the fights and scuffles for a moment, your next-door neighbours were like family and you'd do anything for your friends without question. It was a shitty place but it was our shitty place. I got myself a job in a rock factory and, although the money was crap, I used to have a good laugh with one of my mum's mates, Annie, who also worked there. I would like to say I kept my head down and worked hard, but Annie ended up helping me steal loads of rock to go and sell myself!

But my life was about to take an unexpected turn. That dream I had, that dream of 'doing something big', was about to become a reality. And it all started with a TV show ...

Chapter Three

The farm

'They'll eat you alive Jane, those fucking sharks will eat you alive.'

Frank Smallbone

I COULDN'T take my eyes off the telly. I was mesmerised, 100 per cent completely and utterly transfixed with what I was watching. It was like nothing I had ever seen before and yet, at the same time, something that I felt completely connected to. It is very hard to explain, I had no knowledge of boxing or these two women I was watching and yet right away I saw something that I wanted to do. Something I could do.

'Hell, I could do even better than them,' I thought to myself. It really was as simple and straightforward as that.

My mentality was that as I had always fought with the boys I would be tough enough to do this.

The TV show in question was a documentary show about American boxing star Christy Martin and Irish woman Deirdre Gogarty. And when people say to you, can you remember exactly where you were when your life changed forever? Well, yes, I can absolutely. This was the moment I knew I had a future, I knew I wanted to box and that was that. And not only did I want to box, I wanted to be the best – I wanted to be a champion, I wanted to be on TV! I wanted to be rich and famous and a boxing legend. Straight away, as soon as I saw the girls on the TV in America, I was like, I can beat them. I just knew it.

'I'd be good at that wouldn't I?' I said to Tom; he was back home for a while.

'Yeah, yeah, that'll be right up your street Jane, that.' It was all I needed. Tom thought I could do it too; well, I was going to do it then wasn't I? Turns out he was the only one who did believe in me for a very long time. And I often wonder what would have happened if I hadn't seen that documentary. What if I had been out that evening and missed it … what would I be doing? It really was such a pivotal moment for me and my future was set out the moment I laid eyes on the two women boxers. Until then, I had no clue where my life was headed. Boxing wasn't a goal for me before that moment, it had no bearing on my life whatsoever. Yet I had watched the show and now I wasn't going to do anything else for the next 20-odd years of my life except boxing. I was obsessed.

The very next day I went to the local boxing gym and told them I wanted a trainer, someone to teach me how to box.

And that was met with a moment or two of silence. And then laughter.

'You can't come in here, you're a fucking girl!' came the reply.

And I wasn't sure if they were joking at first. 'But I saw it on the telly last night!'

'Yeah, that was in America,' they said, 'You'll have to go there.'

'Are you fucking joking?' I said. And that was that. Backs were turned, they carried on with what they were doing, I had been told. And again, in all the interviews I have ever given about getting into the sport, about me first trying to train, it was exactly that. No one could give a shit about a woman wanting to box, it wasn't done here and that was that.

The Fleetwood gym I had gone to was run by a bloke called Tommy Norton but there was an old coach in there called Frank Smallbone who trained all the amateur boxers. He was someone that my dad knew so he vaguely knew my family. Dad had gone to see him that day, prepare him that I might be in to see him and that I wanted to box, so when I went in and spoke to him I was hoping for a bit of a lifeline. I wanted to meet one person who wasn't completely and utterly against me.

'I want to box,' I said. And he started laughing.

Frank was in his 60s, he had been training boxers most of his life after taking up the sport himself and he couldn't get his head round what I was saying.

'Ahh, Jane. What you want to do that for? Fucking boys do that,' he said, 'not girls.'

'I've seen it on telly, Frank,' I said. 'I wanna do it, please help me.' To this day I don't know what changed his mind, other than perhaps the fact he had a family connection or he felt sorry for me. Or maybe, even at his age, he knew that things needed to change.

'Come tomorrow night then,' he said. 'Come and join in the training.'

Such simple words. But the implication, what it meant to me, was huge. So I did just that, I went back to the gym the following evening and when I arrived I felt immediately outnumbered and on edge. There were a bunch of blokes there just laughing and egging me on and seeing what the hell I was doing in their territory. The laughter was the worst. Like they were simply putting up with me, pitying me, letting me have a go so I could get it out of my system. I was an amusement to them, nothing else. These guys were serious amateur boxers and they didn't have a clue why I was there or why I wanted to be there – and why the hell I was even allowed there!

And sure, they let me have a go at punching the bag and I hit it well a couple of times, but they were just taking the piss really. The mentality was, 'Oh she'll get fed up in a bit, let her have a little go then she'll get fed up and leave.'

Almost like you'd treat a toddler who is adamant they want to put on their own shoes, even if you know it would just be quicker and easier for everyone involved to do it yourself, you let them have a try. Keep them happy as they'll soon get bored trying. But I didn't get bored of putting on my shoes. It made me more determined than ever I suppose. This was the first time I had ever done anything in my life and felt different. I had been battering and fighting with boys all my life, why the hell was I not allowed to do it now? It made no sense to me, none at all, and I didn't get fed up, I didn't get bored and I didn't quit. I kept going back and it was obvious pretty quickly that I wasn't going anywhere. But Tommy ran the gym and when he came in and started on Frank, I knew it was going to get harder. But Frank, bless him, stood his ground and gave me something that up until that point I hadn't had. Respect.

'She's not going anywhere,' I heard him tell Tommy. 'She can train with the boys.'

But there was no way Tommy was going to allow that. It was too risky, and Frank, one of the top amateur coaches in Fleetwood, couldn't be seen to condone it either. But they knew I wasn't someone who was just going to go away. I was here for the long haul, I was here to learn how to box and I wasn't going to be fobbed off so we made a deal. I would come back when all the other boxers had left and the gym was closed for the night and Frank would train me.

'Don't fucking tell anyone,' he'd warn me, 'I'll get a right fucking name for myself.' And I didn't. I went to see him as much as I could and I absorbed everything he said. A local lad who didn't care who he sparred with, Mark, would get the keys to the gym and we'd sneak in and he and Frank would help me. I'd spar with Mark, and Frank would give me advice about keeping my hands up and doing this or doing that. And I remember clearly how fucking hard it all was. I was so unfit! I hadn't realised until now how out of shape I was. You have to be so athletic and strong to be a boxer. I was just working in a rock factory, making Blackpool rock, I wasn't fit! I did ask the fellas at the factory if I could hang up a punch bag so I could practice, but they couldn't get their heads around it.

'Really Jane?' they said, 'you're fucking mad.' But because of what I had seen with Tom and how he had followed his dream, it gave me hope. That was all I was trying to do, follow my dream, so I just got on with it. I started working at a scrapyard later, which was run by gypsy travellers, and if anyone fell out with anyone or if there was trouble at the yard, bare-knuckle fighting was the only thing that would sort it out. Everyone joined in those fights, including me, but I was using it to learn and to practise. I would have a ruck with anyone if it meant getting training and sparring time.

Tommy stopped me using the gym in the end. There was talk amongst the serious amateurs that Frank was helping me and, because he was such a respected and well-known coach, it was starting to cause problems. He'd been a successful boxer before he became an amateur coach and he didn't want any trouble. Boxing, coaching and training amateurs was his life, he had a fantastic reputation and a very long, successful career in Fleetwood. So I knew that being coached by him, having him on my side, was going to be damaging for him. But I desperately needed him. He was the first person who gave me the time of day, the first person who recognised that I was serious about boxing and didn't care if I was a woman or not. But the amateur world weren't impressed, and they were so outraged he was helping me that they threatened to take away his coaching licence.

That broke his heart. It broke my heart. Who did they think they were? What the hell difference did it make if he was helping me in his spare time? I wasn't taking time away from his amateur boxers, I wasn't getting in the way, I was coming into the gym at night for fuck's sake, training when no one else was around. I wasn't bothering anyone and Frank shouldn't have borne the brunt of it. But he did. He had to leave the gym and they took his licence away. He stood by me and that meant ending his career. He was 60 years old, had given his life to training and coaching some of the biggest amateur boxers in Fleetwood and then suddenly it was all over. All because of me. And the most incredible thing? He stuck by me and never once did he blame me for putting him in this situation.

'I'll stick with yer Jane, it don't matter,' he said. But I knew deep down it did.

On Sunday, 30 October 1994, I took part in my first boxing fight. It was against a policewoman, Kalpna Shah, in Wigan. It turns out this was her second and last time in the ring. I knocked her out in the second round and that was that for her. Who knows, perhaps she decided she'd stick to being a copper after all! I caught the bus to the fight on the night of my debut – glamorous eh? – but I had everyone from the rock factory on the bus too, they all wanted to come and support me. That was unbelievable in itself, the fact they were all behind me, and I sat in the front of the bus, nervous as hell about what my fight would be like, while they had all started drinking and were slowly getting louder and louder as we got nearer. It was even worse on the way home; we had to stop several times for them to get out and have a piss while I was just wanting to get home, tired after the fight and sober as a judge.

I think I must have said after all the run-ins I had with the police in the past, that fighting a copper, knowing I wasn't going to get into trouble for it, was brilliant. Or something to that effect. And it was something the press picked up and ran with for years afterwards. I don't think anyone paid any attention at the time, but I remember it coming back in every interview and every article that was written about me years later. Yes of course I had said something like that, I had just won my first fight, I was probably buzzing, but what sort of picture does it paint of me every time it's brought out and paraded for people to read? This woman likes to punch policewomen? It's not exactly an endearing image is it?

The publicity around the fight wasn't good for Frank either, he was dealing with a lot of crap from everyone questioning why on earth he was helping me train.

'It's out of order!'

'It's disgusting!'

'She shouldn't be allowed to do that!'

'Is she a freak?' They were just the tip of the iceberg.

During my fight with the policewoman in this dingy little nightclub, it was Frank who was making me aware of the dangers of fighting in an underground world. Women's boxing was illegal in this country, no one wanted it and no one did it, except a small group of women, about 30 of us I think there were, in the whole country, who all had to train in secret and just wanted to box. All the matches were arranged between this small group, which made them dangerous. I was training but only had one fight – what if the person brought in to fight me had had 20-odd fights? What was her KO record? Nothing was regulated or checked, and it was all well and good training and then someone arranging a fight for you, but you had no idea about your opponent until you met them, it was insane. You were fucked. Frank was the first to spot this and, coming from his controlled amateur boxing world, he was livid.

'Who you fighting?' he asked.

'I don't know, some copper,' I said.

'How many fights has she had?'

'One.'

'And she won it? You sure she's only had one?'

'That's what they said,' I told him.

It turned out that, in my case, I had been told the truth. She'd had one fight and won one fight but the standard of that fight must have been pretty bad as I just pulverised her. She didn't even hit me, and it was a bit sad really, but I was just battering away and then in the second round it was all finished. One of the other girls who fought after me that night, she got a real pasting. She was beautiful and could have been a model. She had her kids there watching her and she got a broken nose, cheekbone, two black eyes. And there was no way of knowing about her opponent, who they had put her in with. There was no fair fight or balance. Frank was fuming. He knew regulated boxing wasn't like this at all, it would never have been allowed.

'This is just wrong Jane, you'll beat all of these, none of these can fight,'

'What do I do?'

'I don't know,' he said, 'I don't know anything about women's boxing. But it's fucking wrong.' As well as this being my first fight, this night in Wigan was memorable for another reason: it was the night I met Tex, the man who was to become my trainer for the next 15-odd years. He was giving out trophies at the event and he told me about his gym in Bristol. I could train there in secret, he said, I could live on the farm where the gym was and everything I needed would be there, all in one place. He saw all the people I'd brought with me in support, he could see I was popular and I was energetic, he'd help teach me, he said, teach me boxing. Well, that was all I needed to hear.

I had my sights set on Bristol from that moment on. But I had met up with another guy from Fleetwood, a guy called Steve Presnail, who was connected with the town's football club and a big supporter of sport and local athletes, and he said he had a couple more fights lined up for me.

'Fuck, Jane, you're going to get killed if you don't come with me.'

'What you on about Steve?'

'I've seen the fights,' he said. 'I was there in Wigan. Some of those girls took a right battering. It's not fair, come on, come with me, I'll do your shows.' I trusted him with him arranging my matches, even though I knew it still wasn't completely safe. I also knew he was going to do what he could to make sure the fights were fair and as matched as possible. He organised ambulances and doctors to be in attendance, which meant that our safety was at least being taken seriously. He was a great promoter, he put me as the main event and all three of those shows were a sell-out. Steve was really good at organising stuff, and from the day I started he was by my side. It was good to have him. He also worked as a printer so a lot of the publicity posters and flyers were brilliantly done, thanks to him.

Three months after my first fight in Wigan I was back in the ring for my second fight on New Year's Day in 1995. A few months later in April I knocked out my third opponent in the fourth round, and in July that year I boxed against Julia Shirley and won on points. I had four fights and four wins to my name, and although I didn't make any money out of it, I got a bit of experience of being in the ring. And that experience would prove to be invaluable when I was chucked to the lions in the world title fight only a few months later.

Although the fights were illegal, I was under the impression that it wasn't ever something I would be arrested for. A lot of my friends didn't understand it, they couldn't understand why I'd want to do something that could get me into trouble.

'Why don't you just give up boxing?' was such a common question.

'Cos I don't want to,' was my equally common answer.

I was focused on winning more fights and boxing in more venues and that could only happen now if I left Fleetwood and took up Tex's offer of training with him in Bristol. The time had come to say goodbye to Frank. I had to do it, he didn't want me to go, but I couldn't live with the fact his licence had been taken away from him.

'I'm gonna go away Frank, I'm going to go to Bristol.'

'No, no, I'll help you Jane, it's going to be alright. You don't need to go away, they'll fucking eat you alive them sharks in that boxing world.'

'I'll be alright Frank, I'll be OK. There is someone in Bristol who can help me, someone who can train me. You can go back to the gym.'

'No Jane, I'll stay with you, I like it with you.'

'It's fine Frank, honest, I've got someone who can help me now, I'll be OK, honest I will. I'll be alright, I'll come home if there's a problem.' And that was my intention, honest to God, every time there was a problem that was my intention, to just come home. But I never did. I couldn't give in. There was something driving me to keep going, to not admit defeat.

Frank was my first proper trainer, my first proper insight into this new world. He cared about me and I cared about him, which is why I was certain that leaving him was for the best. He would have given it all up for me, but in my mind he had already given up enough.

But I didn't know what I was walking into and he did, he knew the world. He tried to warn me. Sharks eating me alive? That was right as it turned out. He knew how they were all taking the piss out of me at home, he knew it was going to get a lot worse if I kept going and he was trying to protect me.

So I said goodbye to Frank after my fourth fight and I said goodbye to Fleetwood. I'm a great believer that everything happens for a reason. If I had stayed in Fleetwood with Frank, well … who knows. I bet I wouldn't be where I am today and I still don't know if that's a good thing or not! The likelihood is that I wouldn't have got the boxing opportunities I did when I made the move to Bristol. But also, it wasn't like I had much choice – there weren't a lot of options for me if I wanted to carry on boxing. It's not like nowadays, where you can walk into any gym you want and train. I didn't have that privilege!

So you can see why in the end the choice was simple – stay in Fleetwood and hope for a few more underground fights or go to Tex's farm and to his gym and train – and then get good enough to start fighting abroad, in countries like Germany and America, where women were boxing quite openly and legally! I was filled with optimism, hope, focus and excitement. I gave up everything, I gave up my family, my friends, my freedom. Once I had decided to go to Bristol to be the best, that was it, I was completely driven. But I had no real idea of what lay ahead.

Bristol could not have been more different to Fleetwood, which wasn't that hard to fathom as it was a completely different part of the country, but there was so much greenery and space everywhere. Tex had a farm in the middle of nowhere – I am not exaggerating, there was nothing around for miles – it was where he lived and it was on that farm he had built his boxing gym, Spaniorium Farm Gym.

Everything was set up at the farm, it had everything, and pages and pages and pages of boxers all listed to use the facilities for training. I lived in a little house that had been built separately to Tex's main farmhouse, so the gym and the cows were my neighbours. It helped that the farm was so isolated as, although it was very well known in the boxing world, it was secret enough from the public that the big names in boxing could use it unnoticed. Lennox Lewis trained there for his title fight against Frank Bruno; in fact, all the big names were there – Lennox, Frank, Glenn Catley, Dean Francis, plus all the local boxers too. And it was bloody exciting when you saw them, they were like celebrities in a weird sense. I'd gone from fighting on street corners with my mates to sitting on a bench with some of the most recognised faces in boxing. What the fuck?! I was pinching myself to begin with, and then I realised I was here to train and they were here to train. We had a job to do. I wasn't welcomed with open arms, but the boxers there knew I wasn't causing trouble, I just wanted to learn and to train so after a while they settled down to having a woman around. They didn't give me the time of day at first, but they soon realised I was one of them, a fighter, and all boxers have respect for other boxers. They know how hard it is. Of course, I did still have the odd few dickheads who'd try to knock me out in sparring and make it difficult, saying that I shouldn't be using the gym. But probably 80 per cent of the fighters were alright because were all trying to get to the same place – to be a better boxer.

Frank Bruno and Lennox had finished training at the farm when I arrived, but neither of them would have cared about having a woman boxer in the gym. I became good friends with Frank a few years later, and he said he was perfectly sound about me training, although he hated the idea of women boxing. None of them like it. They liked me as a person and showed me respect as an athlete and boxer, but neither of them could quite get it. But that's OK. I realised pretty early on that you can't change people's opinions about you. They let me carry on with my business and that was fine. It's the people who want to stop you doing something because they don't like it, that's what gets me. And I had no idea how much of that attitude was to bulldoze me in the years to come.

My life was now living and breathing boxing. I was living on the farm, waking up and going training. I had no escape from it, and at first it was OK. I was sparring against men day in and day out – I didn't have much choice, it was either that or spar with the imaginary boxer! I could cope with sparring with the lads. I took a lot of punches, I took a lot of knocks but I didn't ever stop. I became used to it and I think that is why I got as tough as I did as quickly as I did. The punches came thick and fast, and in some ways sparring with the blokes meant that they treated me as an equal, I didn't get any special favours or treatment. They'd help me and I'd try to help them in other ways – I might work on their fitness or cardio with them and they'd help me with sparring.

'Come on Jane, we'll do a few rounds with you.' I got that a lot.

We did become a little family I suppose, all training together. I used to spar with one lad, Simon Stowell, and he'd hit me and I'd hit him and he'd hit me back harder. He didn't give a fuck I was a woman.

'I thought that's what you wanted?' he'd say after I took a bit of a battering from him one afternoon. He was right: I wanted equality, in the ring and elsewhere.

All the lads I sparred with, Simon, Eddie Hedges, Luke Clayfield, Darren Dorrington, Chris Long, Dean Cooper, they all made me feel part of something for the first time I suppose. I loved our little wars, our training, our sparring, I was in a bubble. When I first went into boxing, people like me didn't really exist, I was classed as a bit of a nutter. But no one was saying that in the gym, no one was saying it on the farm. It was a big secret that I was there, but I didn't feel any different to any other boxer there training. If I am completely honest, it was the training that got me through the hours of loneliness. And the loneliness was fucking tough. Going from Fleetwood, from a place where you'd know lots of people and there would always be comings and goings, to a farm in the middle of the countryside was brutal. I would wake up on my own, in the silence of the surroundings, and lie there, thinking of my family back in Fleetwood, the place I had longed to escape from for so many years. I had to focus on my training, on the bigger picture, on boxing, on being world champion, but it wasn't easy. I had no money, I couldn't get a job because the training took over my life and I didn't have a car either so if I ever did leave the farm it would be on foot. Not that there was anything around to walk to, other than a phonebox in the village nearby, but even that was a good four-mile hike. I tried cutting across the fields a couple of times but ended up with a whole load of cows and bulls chasing me! I had climbed over the fence and had trudged halfway through the field with its long grass before I caught sight of them out of the corner of my eye, all still as statues they were, all watching me intently. Do I run? Do I carry on walking? Do I try to scare them off? You don't get many cows in Fleetwood so I hadn't got a clue! And I tell you what, I never knew a herd of cattle could move so sodding fast! It was bloody scary but thank goodness I was relatively fit by then and could sprint out over the gate to safety.

And then the other time I decided to cross-country I somehow managed to get completely covered in mud, so when I finally got to the village I was pissed off and in a right state and the locals thought I was some strange-looking thief! Talking to Mum in that cold, piss-smelling phonebox was both a blessing and curse at the same time. I was homesick for her, homesick for her voice, and yet boxing was what I wanted to do and this was where I needed to be. But it was hard. I just didn't let on to anyone how hard it was, and at the first sign of my voice cracking I'd end the call. I didn't want to worry Mum, she didn't need to know how lonely I was. And this was just the beginning.

So, in an effort not to worry Mum, I'd lie, I'd say everything was fine, I'd tell her I was training hard and having a ball. I'd tell her I was learning lots and was enjoying myself. I'd make jokes about where I was and about the locals.

'Oh Mum it's horrible,' I'd say, 'they all talk funny here. Not like us up north. I can't understand a word they're saying!'

'Oh Janey! If you don't like it there love, just come home.'

'Gotta go Mum, the pips are going …' And that was that. And I'd begin my four-mile walk back to the farm. Never home. Always 'the farm'.

Chapter Four

The Fleetwood Assassin

*'An Ode to Fearless Women: Defined by
no man, you are your own story, blazing
through the world. And when they dare tell
you about all the things you cannot be, you
smile and tell them that you are both war
and woman and you can't be stopped.'*

Nikita Gill

'**L**ADIES and gentleman, please give a warm welcome to the British Welterweight Champion! 'It was four weeks before I was due to fly to Copenhagen for my first world title fight, and here I was walking into a television studio for an interview on the *Frank Skinner Show.*

The audience were clapping as I came in from backstage and made my way over to Frank, but I barely registered the noise. I was so nervous. I walked in my normal stompy sort of way, big grin on my face, but unsure where to look – do I make eye contact with Frank, the audience? I was so terrified and in the end I think I walked on with my head down until the last moment when I tilted it towards Frank as I got closer. I think he could tell I was nervous. I was smiling from ear to ear in a very self-conscious way, and I spoke so quietly at first that I think he was worried no one in the studio audience or on TV would hear what I was saying.

'That has shocked you, hasn't it?' he began, turning to the audience. There was no way they were expecting a woman to walk out.

Tex had been drumming up a bit of publicity for me. I had won four out of four of my underground fights before I moved to Bristol and now he had arranged for me to be fighting for a world title. And Frank Skinner, who is a big boxing fan, thought I'd be good for his show.

It was my first-ever TV interview and I had no idea what to expect, I wasn't sure what to say or how to act. The show was recorded over 20 years ago, at the end of 1995, but I remember it like it was yesterday because I was on the show with two icons: Brian London, the British heavyweight champion, and Marvin Hagler, an undisputed fucking legend in boxing. You couldn't even touch that sort of talent, he is the best middleweight boxer to have ever walked the earth and I was in complete awe of him as I sat in the green room backstage. And he was so nice. I was introduced to him as soon as I went in by a guy who worked on Frank's show, and he looked at me with his serious stare that would have struck fear in all his opponents.

'Women box?' he went.

'Yeah,' I said.

'Well good luck to you girl, good luck to you.'

Marvin Hagler, a legend in the boxing world, is one of the best pound-for-pound boxers and he was OK with women boxing. Wow, just wow. I couldn't tell him what that meant to me. He was a real gentleman and when I told him this was my first time in a TV studio, my first live TV appearance, he tried to put me at ease by talking to me right up to the point of going out on stage. Just being on the same show as the likes of Brian and Marvin was such an amazing experience, not to mention a real boost. I was completely blown away, not just by meeting him but by having him validate women's boxing. I was in heaven.

And Brian London, he treated me exactly the same way – with respect. He was fine with me and fine with women's boxing. He even came to one of my fights a few years later. I had a great respect for him.

Frank was good fun and I did relax during the interview after a while. I had never done anything like this before and I was so tense about it. I ended up grinning like a Cheshire cat, blushing a lot and looking up at the ceiling too. I wasn't sure what camera was recording and how loud I had to be. I don't think anyone would recognise that shy, timid girl on that show as the boisterous character that I became a few years later – a character that was created for me by the press and I played along with, but more on that later. I enjoyed Frank's show, I guess being anxious was understandable as this was a world I was completely new to. I was just Jane from Fleetwood, I didn't know anything about chat shows or being on TV! Frank knew I had my world title fight coming up, and as well as asking about training for that we got on to the subject of boyfriends and dating. I won't lie, I am a bit of a flirt, and when I asked him if he was single and he said he was I told him to join me on the sofa! He then snuggled against me for the rest of the interview. Frank was good fun and a decent bloke and I felt good afterwards. I think this was the first time I felt accepted in the boxing world, part of the bubble. It is only a small world and when you are in it, you feel important, you feel you are someone special, someone great, someone who is respected. It would be many years later that I realised what a joke that was.

In my mind back then I thought the whole world knew all the amazing things I was doing because in my little boxing world, in my head, I was amazing. And in my head Marvin Hagler was my mate and would remember my name, but in reality, once Marvin had gone back to Italy and Brian had gone back to Blackpool, they probably wouldn't think fuck all about me. It was a creation of friendship in my brain because we shared the same membership to this small world and that made us all equals.

I bumped into Luke Clayfield the other day, an ABA champion and fit as fuck when I first met him at the farm. I used to stand toe-to-toe with him in training and when we were both sparring he didn't hold back and neither did I; we'd be knocking the fuck out of each other.

He fought Ricky Hatton in the amateurs back then and was very talented. He spent loads of time with me in the gym, teaching me ways to stand, to hold my hands up, to do this or that. He was one of those blokes who was willing to help me, saw past me being female and just saw me as a boxer and I was so grateful. They all had that respect for me and I respected them. It was everyone else that was the problem!

Training was pretty intense leading up to the title fight. I had four unlicensed matches to my name, which was no preparation for a world title. But I didn't know that at the time; the level of fighting I had seen in just my four fights was, for want of a better word, shit. The women I'd fought in England were crap, no one could touch me, I was arrogantly sure of that. So, of course, when Tex came to me asking me if I wanted to take on a world welterweight title, I was raring to go.

'Yeah fuck it, let's go to Denmark, let me fight the world champion!' I said to Tex, with all the bravado and naivety of a fighter with only four fights to her name. I knew my opponent Sandra Geiger's history – she had 29 fights and 29 knockouts – but that didn't stop me believing I would be the one to beat her.

'Watch out, Sandra, here comes the Fleetwood Assassin,' I would wake up and say to myself. I was so determined, I think that's sometimes my problem, I was like a dog with a bone. I still am with certain things. I couldn't focus on anything else but getting that world light-welterweight title, it was an obsession, a fixation, a goal, but not in a healthy sense because it was pure, blind bravado. I hadn't watched Sandra fight before, I hadn't studied her matches and seen her weaknesses.

Now I look back and think it was a wonder I wasn't killed in the ring. I honestly can't believe that someone like me with so little experience – a measly four fights – and only a few months of training should have been allowed to fight a champion boxer like that.

And if I am honest, it was only the lads in the gym who got me through that fight. It got postponed a couple of times, which was frustrating at the time but turned out to be a blessing in disguise. Every time the date got moved back I had more time to prepare, more training time with the boys, more sparring time, more coaching. I hated being at the farm, living in a place so far removed from what I would ever call home. But I had to tell myself that this was where I needed to be in order to make a name for myself in the boxing world. This is where I needed to be if I wanted to be a world champion. I had trained for nine months solid, three times a day, no time for friends or a job or anything else. I was just focused on winning this title, to compete at a world level.

I wanted it more than anything.

My confidence and bravado flew with me out of Bristol but promptly disembarked when we landed in Denmark. I wasn't in the best of moods when we landed as I was so hungry and getting grumpy. Tex and Steve were with me; Steve had helped with my promotion of this fight so it was a big deal for him as well as me.

The weigh-in happened pretty much as soon as we landed, which was a blessing as I was starving. You had to be so strict with your diet, I couldn't eat anything that day except a few rice cakes, and my plan was to stuff my face straight after the weigh-in. To compete for the world light-welterweight championship title I had to be ten stone, and I was. Sandra was there at the weigh-in, professional and poised as the press surrounded her. She didn't speak very good English but she made her feelings clear when it came to the photocall after we had our weights confirmed. She was sticking her face right out and up to me then. It was a clear and aggressive message: I was no one, she was world champion, that wasn't going to change.

The press were all over us as she was such a big name, all the photographers and promoters wanted lots of photos and lots of quotes from her because she was such big news. I hadn't seen any of her fights before but I knew she was from a judo and kickboxing background. I think she had done everything. But, honest to God, all I could really think about, now that I had had my weigh-in, which had taken longer than I was expecting because of who I was fighting, was that I could finally eat! I had literally starved myself that day and now I just wanted to stuff myself and get some sleep.

Tex, Steve and I went to get the key for our hotel room and then we could collect our meal vouchers from reception.

'Sorry, the vouchers are only for the fighters.'

'Yes, I am a boxer on the show.'

Silence.

'I am boxing for the world title.'

Silence. Then: 'These meal vouchers are only for the male fighters.'

And that was that. I had no money with me, and although I had Steve and Tex with me it felt like we were complete outcasts. This wasn't what any of us were expecting and not what I imagined we'd be treated like. I was due to box on TV the following night, on one of the biggest TV channels in Denmark.

Our title fight was the warm-up fight to the Danish boxer Brian Nielsen, who was a massive star in Denmark with an unblemished record. So even though Sandra and I were boxing for a world title, we were only the warm-up act, as it were, for Nielsen who was fighting American boxer Mike 'The Bounty Hunter' Hunter. Compared to their fight, compared to the men, we weren't expected to provide much entertainment other than filling the slot before the main event. Why would two female fighters need food vouchers, eh?

Denmark was expensive, I had no money but Steve helped me out. It was his night too, he had put a lot of work into getting me here and he wanted it to work as much as I did.

That night I tried and failed miserably to get a good night's sleep. I couldn't seem to switch off. I was thinking about food – or lack of food! – and the crap we'd had to deal with, and in the end I just got fed up of lying in bed awake so decided to go for a little wander. It wasn't exactly ideal preparation for a world title fight, but I needed to do something so I crept out of my room and through the stairwell door, which was right next door. I went down a flight of steps before I could smell cigarette smoke and there, sitting down on the steps only a few feet away was only the bloody Bounty Hunter! I couldn't believe my eyes, he was due to be fighting for his own world title tomorrow and was a much more experienced fighter than me, so what the hell was he doing out in the stairwell having a fag in the middle of the night?

'Are you not boxing tomorrow?' I said to him. I figured I would keep him company for a bit and he didn't seem to mind when I sat down next to him.

'Yeah,' he said. 'Are you not boxing?'

'Yeah,' I replied. 'I'm boxing a French girl,' I said.

'Ahh, right,' he said, having another toke on his fag. 'I'm boxing the main event ... Nielsen,' he said. I knew who Nielsen was, he was a Danish heavyweight world champion and he was fighting tomorrow to retain his IBO heavyweight title. Nielsen was a big name, a big star and a fierce fighter. I wasn't too sure what preparation he would have done for the fight but I was pretty sure smoking the night before wasn't anywhere on his training schedule.

'Why are you smoking?' I asked him.

'Well, I'm not here to win,' he said. Like it was the most simple, straightforward explanation in the world. And I didn't have a clue what he was talking about. What did that mean? He was due to be fighting in the headline fight tomorrow, the main event, he was the big challenger for Nielsen's belt ... I didn't get what the hell he meant.

'Well, why are you here then?' I said. 'What do you mean?' It made no sense to me and I didn't care whether that was because I was still a bit of a novice in this world, I needed to understand.

He got up then, cigarette finished, and walked back up the steps to the door.

'Watch and see,' he said. And that was that.

The fight itself was held at the K.B. Hallen, a place Tex knew well as he had boxed there when he was in the RAF in the 50s, and there were TV cameras and crew everywhere, lighting rigs, people with clipboards, people with ear mics, it was mad. But the madness was only just beginning. Geiger was a huge star in France, and although I knew of her successful boxing history I had no idea of the level of her fame until the night of our fight.

The French president Jacques Chirac had flown in with an array of official-looking statesmen and ambassadors and the atmosphere was very much geared up to celebrate and applaud their big star. Of course it was a big deal to her, and to them, but to me, well, it was all a bit bloody surreal. She'd been here before, she knew what to expect, how to act, she had all the media training. In the press conference beforehand I know I came across as a novice little minnow compared to her world-champion-big-fish status, but that wasn't my fault. I hadn't had any media training, I couldn't really understand what they wanted me to say when the questions were fired at me: 'Do you realise Geiger has won ...'

'Why do you want to fight the undefeated ...?'

'Do you know she hasn't ever ...?'

Yeah, yeah, yeah. I had no interest in doing interviews and talking the talk, I just wanted to beat her. I wanted to get into the ring and show her what I could do.

When I walked out towards the ring, Steve led the way, acting as standard-bearer carrying the Union Jack. I am not sure what the crowd were expecting but I was smiling, bouncing up and down, throwing round a few punches as I made my way to the ring, and then I had to wait for Geiger to make her entrance. I started shadow-boxing whilst I waited and I could see some of the audience looking on in bewilderment. It was almost as if they were thinking what the hell is this English woman doing? Perhaps they felt a bit sorry for me; a lot of Geiger's fans had seen her demolish her opposition, I think they might have thought I was just a hyperactive plaything for their champion to toy with for a few rounds before she got bored. They were just laughing at me, they all thought I was a little muppet from England who would get knocked out in one of the early rounds and that would be that. She was a fearsome puncher and yet I didn't know that, I didn't have a clue but the crowd did. They all knew what I was about to face, they were all on her side, all part of her boxing history, and knew what had happened to her previous opponents.

And then all of a sudden she was in the ring and all these people were in there too, all giving her flowers and treating her like she had already won the fight! I felt completely invisible as I stood there looking on. I was being completely ignored and, if anything, this over-the-top adulation of my opponent, just yards from me before I had even thrown a punch, just added fuel to my fire.

If the crowd treated her with respect because of her boxing record they still didn't quite accept that women's boxing was on a par with the main event later that evening. There wasn't a great deal of respect. There was a lot of laughing as we had walked in, it was quite obvious. A crowd was gathering but it was still early if you'd come to see the big heavyweight match later. The fact that we were being allowed to box on a major TV network on the undercard of a massive fight was still something though, I thought. It was getting recognition in this country and it was legal to have women fighting, but there was still so much humour to it.

The fight itself? Well, the only way to describe it is brutal.

Steve was nervous, Tex was nervous, they were all watching the spectacle of Sandra being fawned over as if the fight was just an inconsiderate blip and there was no other outcome but for her to win.

'I don't care what she's done in the past,' I said to them before the bell went, 'I'm not going down!'

Well, it was true at first. In the first round, I didn't go down. But my fighting was terrible. I couldn't even box at the time, not really. I wasn't as skilled or as technical as her, but I just didn't give up. I kept going and going and going and going.

In the second round I took a hard knock and was left badly dazed and confused. I was trying to stay up on my feet but she hit me so hard and just kept hitting me and hitting me. I grabbed on to the ropes and was holding on, I was just about still on my feet but I was like a drunk trying to remain balanced and I was quickly losing that battle. I was completely out of it. The bell had gone, it was the end of the round and I stumbled back to the corner with absolutely no idea where I was. Was I in Fleetwood? What was happening? But I sat there, trying to get my head out of the haze and back in the ring. Even after the minute, I still could feel the effect of that punch but I just carried on. I stood up and went back for more. I just didn't give up. I just kept walking on to the punches, walking on again and again and I'm sure they were all thinking, 'What's holding her up?!' I could hear the crowd roaring and I could hear this clapping going on too, it was a really slow, deliberate clap and I was furious.

'They're fucking slow clapping!' I said to Steve when I went back to the corner the next time. 'Why are they slow clapping? Is it shit?'

'No, no Jane, that's what they do when they are enjoying it,' shouted Steve. 'They are loving it.'

And they were, the slow clap was getting louder and louder, and while I was thinking that was signalling they were bored, they were really getting into the fight now. The things you learn as you're being punched in the head! And apart from the clapping, there was a voice I kept hearing clear as day every time I went back in from my corner – a voice I had only properly heard several hours earlier in the stairwell at the hotel – Mike The Bounty Hunter cheering me on. He was so loud and I heard his voice above all the rest of the shouting; he was calling out, 'Bolo Jane, Bolo!' He wanted me to throw her a bolo punch; he kept saying it over and over again. And I think if I had stopped to think that one of the fighters who was the headline fight that night was ringside cheering me on, I probably would have lost the fight due to shock. How cool was that, to have him cheering me on?! And I didn't lose. I broke Geiger's heart in the end with sheer grit, determination and relentlessness. It was too much for her, she couldn't keep going. I think she thought she had won in the second round when I nearly went down, but I just didn't give up, I kept going and punching and she didn't like that. She didn't like me one bit, she just thought she'd knock me out and then she'd go home, like she had done to all her other opponents, but I was a different story. I had won with heart over skill.

We both ended up in hospital after that fight, the pair of us had broken ribs and broken cheekbones, and I had a fractured eye socket, broken jaw and a tooth missing. You see why I said it was brutal? It really was, it was dangerous. It's a wonder I survived. I still don't know to this day why the referee didn't stop the fight in the second round. I was wobbling all over the place, I couldn't stand up properly, I was swaying and staggering like a drunkard and they let it carry on.

It went to the full ten rounds in the end. And then it was down to the judges. I was told, and later learnt over the years, that whenever it goes to a judges' decision it isn't good news for the away fighter as they tended to side with the home boxer. But they couldn't not give it to me as I won every single round – even the second round when she nearly killed me.

My whole body felt like it was on fire as we both staggered back to the referee in the middle. He gripped both of our wrists and started speaking in Danish, and I didn't understand a bloody word. Then he repeated himself in English. 'And the new ...'

That was it, I heard the word 'new' I didn't need to hear anything else, I went mental! I was broken and battered and all of a sudden it was all worth it! I had won on points, I had won every round, and I, Steve and Tex just couldn't believe it! The crowd, who had laughed when we had come on and slow clapped their way through the fight, were now in full roaring mode. They appreciated a bloody, scrappy and hard-fought fight and I felt like a god.

It turned out to be the best fight of the night, this spectacle of a world champion having the heart and soul knocked out of her by a relentless English woman who just kept going back for more, who wouldn't give up.

Before I went to hospital I was adamant that I wanted to return the favour to Mike and watch his fight, and also because I wanted to understand what he meant in the stairwell the night before. I watched his fight even though I was all battered and in pain and I knew I'd be heading to hospital quite quickly afterwards, but I wanted to see the fight for myself. I watched it but I still didn't understand. Nielsen was good, he was tough, but Mike could have beaten him easily. It was like he wasn't really trying, his heart wasn't in it. His level of fitness was definitely questionable, he was there but he wasn't really there, and it was such a mismatched fight in the end. It was like Nielsen was fighting someone who couldn't be bothered and Mike stopped the fight in the fifth round with an injury to his arm.

I still didn't get it, I had just boxed my guts out as the pre-show event, expecting my fight to be just the tantalising taster to surely what would be a meaty and action-packed main event. And, well, it just wasn't. I went to hospital when Mike stopped the fight, and Nielsen looked like he was peeved that he didn't get any sort of proper fight back but he had retained his title and that was that.

I met up with The Bounty Hunter after I came back from hospital, and although I could only just about see out of one eye and the painkillers were helping but not brilliant, I still wanted to find out what had happened. I wanted to understand what was going through his mind, what I had just witnessed. It made no sense to me, this man who looked like he was toying with Nielsen to begin with then sort of just gave up.

'I'm just here for the money Jane,' was his reply. 'I've not trained for ages, I'm not in great shape, I'm just here for the money.'

'But you could have beaten him easily!' I said. I wasn't letting this go. 'You were only playing with him!'

This was my first experience at a proper fight, in a proper event that wasn't a nightclub in Wigan or back in Fleetwood. Hunter was a talented boxer but just didn't seem to care ... he seemed to have lost all his fight.

And I could not have been closer to the truth.

'I'm not interested anymore,' he said. 'I'm not fit enough and I don't want to be fit enough anymore for this shit game. It's a shit game Jane, you'll find out all about it.'

And that was that. He didn't ever fight again after that match and he died just ten years later at 46 years old. That wasn't without its controversy either, he was shot by two policemen on top of his apartment block in LA when he supposedly launched an unprovoked attack on them. I don't know the ins and outs of his death other than when I heard about it, it just seemed like a huge waste of talent – such a waste. And yet if I hadn't met him on the stairwell that night before our fights, I probably wouldn't have been given the insight to the world I was just entering.

And now I was world light-welterweight champion! It was like my whole existence had built up to this one moment – me, Jane Couch, had finally done something phenomenal. I was a champion! I was going to go back to

England and everyone would see what I had done, what a battle I had fought, what an unstoppable athlete I was and everyone would worship me. Everything would change, I thought, they will make women's boxing legal and everyone will celebrate me.

The night before we were due to fly back, I don't think Steve or I could sleep, we were both so excited. I remember saying to Steve on the plane, 'God, look at the state of me, I can't get off the plane like this, all the press are going to be waiting for me!'

I had a swollen black eye so when we landed Steve bought me some sunglasses so I could look half decent when I spoke to all the reporters and the waiting paparazzi. But Tex was quiet, he knew this wasn't ever going to be the case.

'Don't get your hopes up Jane,' he said.

I couldn't fathom why he'd say something like that. Perhaps he didn't want me to get too complacent in training, too big for my boots that I had a world title to my name and maybe I wouldn't work as hard in the gym. It made no sense to me what he said and it pissed me off. I deserved to be excited.

'Whatcha mean? I'm fucking world champion Tex! Do you know how many people become world champion in their lives? I just took on a fucking French monster!'

'I know Jane, but listen …'

But I didn't listen. I was convinced I would be mobbed when I landed back in England. Treated like a champion, a hero. I thought I had done something amazing, something incredible, the stuff that Hollywood films like *Rocky* were based on. Me, a novice female with guts and spirit who had come from nothing, no boxing experience and only four previous fights to her name, and had taken on a legend in the world of female boxing and won! Rags to riches, zero-to-hero, an epic battle from the Fleetwood Assassin!

But there was no one. You know when you see the Olympic athletes come off the plane or the England football team land at the airport there is so much waving and smiling and cheering? I had no one. No one was there, there was no greeting, no media fanfare, no excitement, no congratulations, no press coverage. I was still sore from every single punch I had taken, every hit, every contact and nobody cared.

The most hurtful snub came from the *Boxing News*. There wasn't even a single line from them about my fight. They reported on all the male fights that had happened on the same night as my fight, even the pitiful Nielsen versus Hunter fight – all of those matches got a mention but not mine. And it was such a brutal, ball-breaking, bloody fight – for a world title! – and yet there was no mention of Sandra or myself.

I wasn't standing for that, I was still high on adrenaline and war wounds, so I asked them – I had no qualms about it – why there was not one single mention of my fight. The response? The *Boxing News* only reports on male fights. That was it.

'Bastards,' I thought.

I was completely and utterly deflated. Devastated. I had trained for nine months solid, fighting all the big-name blokes in training, and I'd taken shots after shots in the sparring ring to prepare, starved myself and given up my life, and yet nothing. It didn't mean anything to anyone, only me.

I think I got paid around €1,000 for the fight, but once Tex had taken out money for the hotel room and flights I probably got around €200. Hardly worth the effort really, was it? Of course, I did receive the coveted WIBF belt. For the first six months I kept it with me constantly, I never let it out of my sight. I slept with it, I wouldn't go anywhere without it but no one knew what it was, what it meant.

All I wanted was for the boxing world to acknowledge me, for them to go, 'Oh my God, here is a woman who has trained her arse off and won a world title on her fifth fight.' If a man had done that, he would have been a hero, wouldn't he? He would have been celebrated, wouldn't he?

I would have happily died in that fight, that is how much I wanted it, that is how much it meant to me. I can't believe it when I admit that now. It's hard to write that, to accept that is truly how I felt, not even fearing death if it meant I had done something as incredible as winning the world title.

I took some time out after that fight and went back to Fleetwood.

'Oh love, look at the state of you!' Mum was completely shocked. She thought I was off my head wanting to box and now her worst fear had come true, I had been completely battered.

'I'm alright Mum,' I told her. 'And I won!'

'I don't like seeing you like this Jane, it's not right.'

'S'OK Mum, really, I'm fine. I'm tough!'

And then I started to laugh. If it was our Tom her reaction would have been a lot worse, much, much worse! Tom wasn't tough like me, we both knew it!

So I took the belt home and I enjoyed showing it off a bit. Home was where I had support, I had done three fights there so I had a little following, as it were. People were impressed and the local paper ran a little story on me too. That then got picked up by some of the national papers, but instead of celebrating their home-grown champion the article was more about women boxing and why it was allowed to happen and who watches it and why would they want to do it ... I stopped reading in the end. I was still recovering from the injuries and when I read this shit, I just thought, 'Fuck it, fuck the lot of them.'

I went round to see Frank with the belt and he was over the moon. He was proud of me, he said, and so happy. I told him the belt wasn't just mine, it belonged to him as well, he was my first proper trainer, he believed in me and gave me the chance when no one else did.

'Here comes the Fleetwood Assassin,' he'd say when I turned up to train, after-hours in his gym when everyone else had gone home. And the name certainly stuck! It didn't matter that the majority of my title-fight training had been spent slogging away in Bristol, he was the one who took me in in that very first instance and guided me.

It was brilliant to show him my belt and see him so proud. I could tell it meant as much to him as it did to me. I carried on going home after every fight in the years to come to see Frank. He'd want to know who I'd been training with, what they were teaching me, all sorts of technical questions and he wanted to know everything. I told him the good bits, not about the loneliness or how unhappy I was there.

'See Jane, if you'd stayed with me you wouldn't be doing this, you're with the big boys now! Who've you been sparring? Tell me, who've you met this week?'

And I'd sit happily for hours with him, telling him all about the professional boxers in the gym, all the lads I was training with, what I had learnt.

I told him about the travellers I'd be fighting from the local travellers' site too, how they'd all come into the gym and want to spar with anyone. There was one guy in particular, 'king of the gypsies' he was called, and he'd come in with his gang and they just wanted to fight.

'Anyone want to spar, anyone want to spar ...' that was their usual chant as they came in.

'Yeah I will,' I said.

'But you're a girl.'

'Yeah. But I'll spar with you.' And that was that.

Frank was incredulous to this but he also knew me well, so he knew I'd be taking every opportunity to fight if it meant improving. So I'd fight and I wouldn't hold back, and the next time they came in they'd just ask for me and if I wasn't there they'd wait for me to come back. It was fine with me, it meant more sparring time, more experience. And it was good bloody experience too. They would be going for it, they didn't go easy on me, what would that prove?

None of my fights at that time were technical. My fight with Geiger wasn't technical or pretty, it was just pure guts and determination. I knew I had to improve my technique and learn how to fight properly but that would come over time.

And I was determined to get the title but now ... it just felt like a massive let down. Everything felt pointless. I was fed up with boxing. I did what I set out to do, what was the point of carrying on?

Chapter Five

A fighter not a quitter

*'The strongest people are not those who
show strength in front of others, but those
who win battles we know nothing about.'*

Jonathan Harnisch

I WAS lying on the bed but I didn't get up. I was awake
but I didn't want to be. I couldn't seem to summon
any sort of energy. I was Jane Couch, Fleetwood
Assassin, world light-welterweight champion, but so what?

I just wanted to be home, to be Jane, to be out with
my mates or watching TV with Mum or listening to Tom
and his band play. I wanted to be anywhere but here, on
the farm, living a groundhog day existence.

The problem with wanting something so badly is you
have to have it no matter the cost. And when you are in that

state of mind, you don't see anything wrong with how you are acting or how you are living. You're focused, you can't see the wood for the trees. But now, dear God, now I do. Training for my first title fight against Geiger was all-consuming and yet I felt I had been sucked into this big bubble, this tornado, and I was rising and rising with each training stint and each sparring session and I was at the top now, I had won my title fight, I had done it ... and then all of a sudden the wind dropped. The tornado stopped spinning and I was thrown aside.

Taking time out in Fleetwood after the Geiger fight proved to be my saving. I was healing. I had fractured ribs, fractured cheekbones, broken jawbone ... I'm not glamorising it, it takes a long time for those injuries to heal. And they are painful, of course they are, it's not a quick recovery – physically or mentally. Hand on my heart, there was a huge part of me that was ready to give it all up. I had won the world title after five fights, what else was there to do? I had done what I set out to do, OK, it had happened quicker than I expecting ... so should I carry on? My boxing career can't just be over that quickly now, or can it?

And then Tex got a phone call. Did I want to defend my world title against an American boxer called Andrea DeShong in New Orleans? And can you guess what my first reaction was when he told me? Fucking ... hell ... no. I didn't think I could go through that pain again, I honestly didn't. Andrea was bigger, stronger and more experienced than me and I just didn't think I had it in me.

Not what you expected to hear? Sorry, the brash, bravado, ball-breaking Jane wasn't in the room then. I felt like a broken shell and I honestly couldn't see myself fighting again – let alone a heavier, more powerful boxer than before.

But time, as they say, is a great healer. And it did heal, in a lot of ways. A few weeks went by and I started to feel a bit better. I was recovering from my injuries and I was recuperating well. I was still with my mum in Fleetwood when I made the decision to go back to the farm. It's funny when I think about it, my story could well have stopped there. I could have been satisfied with my belt, my world title and just thought to myself, 'Right then, that's boxing done, what next?'

I would never have gone on to defend my title, to win four more titles, to fight for a change in the law, to make history … These sorts of moments in your life are strange because the decisions you make at the time are based on such simple ideas. Did I want to fight again? Yes, OK, time to go back to the farm. And now I think to myself, whoa, how different my life would have been if I had told Tex to shove his New Orleans fight.

So I accepted the challenge, my injuries from Geiger's fight were a memory now and a boxing match to defend my title was a big pull. It will be different this time, I told myself, there will be more money in this fight, more promotion. This will change things.

I was back in the gym nine months after my world title fight and back in the most intensive training schedule I had ever faced once again. A lad called Stu McKenzie had joined the farm, he'd just turned up one day saying he was a trainer and offered to help. He was a genuine bloke and was so supportive, right from the word go. He would pay out of his own pocket to travel abroad and be in my corner with Tex at the fights. Blokes like that, who just want to help and champion you, give you their time, are worth their weight in gold and his support meant a lot. He was well aware that I had to keep my profile low but that I had to keep training harder than ever. Women's boxing in England, well, it was still an underground activity so I had to keep my head down and keep focused. But Tex, he had other ideas. He liked the publicity, he liked the fact that he had someone like me with him, someone who wasn't afraid to battle in the ring and was likely to get results. Plus I was a world champion now, I had a bit of credit to my name. So he started inviting the press round, a few journalists here and there, a few photographers ... I didn't realise at the time that it was benefitting him more than me, I just used to go along with it, pose for a few photos, answer a few questions and then try to politely get on with my training! But Tex did what he did because it was good for his gym, it was good publicity for his place. I didn't mind but when the 'freak' comments started and the sharks started circling, I didn't know what to do, so I would turn to Tex for help but couldn't help but feel he was the one orchestrating a lot of it. I became dependent on him, convinced he was the one who would protect me and just let me get on with boxing – which, to be fair, was what I signed up for at the time. So he started controlling more and more of my life until I felt unwavering loyalty to him, I didn't even go home anymore. I would want to go back up north but then he'd plant a seed and say things and I thought I had better not rock the boat with him, the man who took me in and gave me somewhere to live and somewhere to train. Who was I to argue when he didn't want me to go back to Fleetwood. He obviously knew what was best for me. But it was all about control, plain and simple.

'Oh you don't want to go back home,' he'd say. 'You go back there and you'll get back on the drink …'

'No I won't, I might have a few nights out but I've worked fucking hard …'

But he had sown that seed and in the end I wasn't going home. I was at the farm, training then fighting then training then fighting. I had no social life, no time to go out, no time to get a job. When I was young, I was a very hyperactive child and my mum used to take me to the doctors to find out if there was anything that could be done to help. The problem was, I'd be going to bed at midnight and waking up at 4am, full of energy and full-on, it would drive her up the wall. But in those days the usual explanation was that I was just a hyperactive child, I'll grow out of it, there isn't anything to be done. So Mum was told that and that was it, you believed it and accepted it and life just carried on. I'd be constantly awake, jittery and hyper, but it didn't matter as I'd grow out of it. Tex, he was the same. He was telling me something, telling me how to behave and at the time I just accepted it. Yes, I should just stay at the farm, it was for the best, just like Mum had accepted my hyperactivity was just a phase when I was younger. Nowadays I reckon I would be classed as having ADHD, Attention Deficit Hyperactivity Disorder. My poor concentration at school and my difficulty in learning, down to ADHD. Of course, I'm not saying that things would have turned out any differently, but it's funny to think about isn't it? What if I'd had some sort of medication or therapy or monitoring, like children with the condition get now? Would my life be any different?

I felt Tex persuading me not to travel home and see my family because I should be focusing on my career, were all subtle ways of controlling me. And that's what it felt to me, was all about; control over my training, over my fighting, over my publicity and it was all done with me being aware of it but not fully aware. I was living it and accepting of it because I believed that is just what happened.

I guess the point I'm trying to make is that sometimes you just accept things as they are, you accept what you're told and that's that. I think back now and get so cross with myself for not leaving the farm. Why did I continue to stay in a place I was so unhappy? I had accepted that Tex knew best so I went with that.

Besides, I needed him. I had to defend my title and he was my trainer.

The New Orleans fight was on a big stage and was being shown on the ABC network, so there was a part of me that thought, naively, that England might pick it up and show clips.

If Geiger's fight was brutal from both sides, my match with Andrea was all about wanting something more than the other person. And I did want it, I wanted to defend my title, I had spent the previous 12 weeks working my arse off training and sparring and I wanted to win. The belt was mine, I wasn't going to let it go easily.

Have you ever heard of Matthew Saad Muhammed? He was one of the best fighters of his era, a WBC light-heavyweight champion and called Miracle Matthew because he kept going in a fight, he wouldn't give up and he had some amazing comebacks when he was in the ring. When we arrived in New Orleans I needed to go to a gym, to do a bit of a pre-fight workout. If you've travelled a long way you need to be able to go somewhere and do a bit of moving about. You've done all the training and all the prep, this is just to keep yourself limber and loose. So we went into this gym and I clocked him straight away.

Well, not straight away, I kept looking over at him thinking, I know this face … I know this face … I was really hot on all boxers past and present so I recognised him, I just couldn't quite remember his name. Then someone said, 'That's Matthew Saad Muhammed.' And I was just, 'Fuck! Yes, that's him!'

I went over to him and introduced myself. We started chatting and although I knew he wasn't boxing then, he was still involved in the game and he told me he had come over from Philadelphia to New Orleans to train up some fighters. He needed to earn a living, he said, he had been living, surviving perhaps I should say, on the streets in Philadelphia. How could this legend, this absolute legend, be homeless I thought to myself? I hadn't got a clue how it could happen, in all honestly I probably didn't want to think how it could happen. But I knew I wanted to help him in any way I could; he was boxing and winning titles when I was growing up, I didn't want to think of what future lay ahead of him if his training didn't go to plan. His situation was so sad and it broke my heart seeing him, knowing what an icon he had been, so I asked the promoter for some extra tickets for my fight. I got a whole load anyway, and I gave them to Matthew, and he was able to sell them all and make himself a bit of money. It wasn't much but it was something, I could help in some small way and that felt right. He came to my fight too, along with another huge name in the boxing world, Angelo Dundee. When I say huge, they probably don't get much bigger than Angelo, he was a world-class trainer and trained one of the greatest sporting legends of all time, Muhammad Ali. Yep, Ali's trainer – who also trained Matthew and Sugar Ray Leonard – was at my fight. And not just at my fight, they both ended up being in my corner with Tex! All the while I was battling DeShong I had the most amazing people waiting for me in my corner and it was such a buzz. How freaking cool is that, knowing that this man, who had trained Muhammad Ali, was waiting for me when the bell rang out. And he was such a good bloke, such a decent man and I was just made up that he was in my corner.

All my fights were pretty similar then, I was too brave for my own good. I fought with my heart rather than skill and I was a brawler. I wasn't a brilliant technical boxer but I was a brilliant brawler and I didn't give up. As I got older I learnt how to box and I learnt how to stop the punches, but in those days I was just hoping that my strength, determination and dogged spirit would get me through and half the time it did! I won that match in the seventh round after DeShong's defence was weakening and my enthusiasm was erupting. After a meaty combination of punches, the referee took her aside to start a standing count before deciding that she was done. I had won. I was buzzing then, this was a big fight, I was on a big TV network in America and I was due to be paid $5,000 for my trouble. After the fight I took part in a press conference and spoke about my love of fighting but that I wished I could do it legally in my own country. I didn't have a clue if anyone would take notice or give a shit but it was a point worth saying. Tex told me that I had been offered £10,000 to fight at Wembley, which of course we had to turn down because of the law. That wasn't right, was it? Fighting abroad wasn't the end of the world but I wanted to stand up in a ring in England and win titles. Besides, once we got paid for this fight, once you take out flights and hotel rooms, you're not left with a lot!

Only, I didn't get paid. The promoter ripped us off and I didn't get a single dollar. 'There's no money,' he said, 'we lost money on the show and we can't pay you.'

I was furious I had come over to defend my title, I did what they asked of me, I had fought and kept my side of the bargain, and now I wanted the money I had rightly worked for. But Tex was adamant there wasn't anything he could do and I was fuming.

'You're my manager, sort it out, go in and get my money!' I told him. 'I've just done my job, I've done what has been asked of me.'

And I started to realise no one really cared about you in this business. Even the ones you thought did. It was no skin off Tex's nose, he wasn't getting battered and bruised. He was still bringing in a fighter, promoting his gym, managing a defending champion. And here I was, borrowing money left, right and centre to be able to train, to be able to eat, to survive. I had bought myself some chickens that I kept at the farm so I could eat their eggs. I was surviving, just, and yet I do the job Tex wanted me to do, and that I was told I would get good money for, and nothing.

The silver lining to being over in New Orleans was going out and hitting the town with Matthew, Angelo and his wife after my fight. I had an absolute blast. New Orleans is such a vibrant, full-on place and we were out in the French quarter and visited jazz bar after jazz bar. It was one of the best nights ever, just so much fun, to experience this part of the country with the people I was with was like a dream come true for me. I didn't want the night to end and when I said bye to Matthew, with a promise to keep in touch, I really meant it. He told me he'd try to come over to England some time and I think my last words to him were something like, 'Make sure you do!' But he never did and I never saw him again. It was an age before social media and Facebook and it was genuinely hard to keep in contact. Of course, there are always ways but the short story is, we didn't, and when I heard about his death I think I will always regret not keeping in contact. His career as a trainer was short-lived and not very successful, and although he had tried to make a go of it he ended up back on the streets in Philadelphia before becoming involved in charity work in the area, which focused on raising money for the homeless. He ended up dying in a hospital in Philadelphia, I am not sure they knew how he died, only that he was 59 years old. That's no age is it? And to have those few days with him was made even more special. No amount of money could buy you that experience, it was just pure luck I suppose that he was there in that gym the day I arrived in New Orleans. And to spend time with him in the gym, and then at my fight, in my corner … and this was a true champion! He could beat me with one hand behind his back! It was one of those moments I will never forget.

And that is where boxing really gets you. One minute it's taking everything from you with a solid punch, you are working your arse off for it, training and then not getting paid when you do fight, and then on the other hand it gives you the opportunity to hang out and absorb the advice and brilliance of some of the greatest names in the game. Talk about conflict. I remember someone telling me once that you should never regret a day in your life because on your good days you're happy, bad days you get life experience, shit days are for learning lessons and the best days give you the best memories. I think when it comes down to boxing, you do get your fair share of shit, so having moments of hanging out with greatness makes it bloody worthwhile. For me to meet these people, especially Angelo Dundee who is, well, a fucking legend! And I almost forgot, he got me through my weigh-in with DeShong too. When it was time for the dreaded weigh-in, I got on the scales, I was a pound overweight. I had to be 140lbs and I was 141lbs. Tex told me to go to the toilet while he demanded a re-weigh, which is a fairly common thing to do before you get your boxer to skip it off to lose the weight. It didn't look good for the trainer to have their boxer not bang-on for the weigh-in. So I went to the toilet and Angelo's wife was in there. She asked me what was wrong and I told her I was a pound overweight. I'd have to lose a pound otherwise I wouldn't be able to fight. And what happened next, well, you couldn't make it up. We came out of the toilets together and she shouted over to Angelo and told him the problem. I was just standing there, looking like a bit of a spare part and not really knowing what was going on.

'Weigh this girl again,' he said to the inspector. 'Jane come here,' he said, 'get back on the scales.' So I did exactly as I was told and got back on the scales and he produced this big tin of peas, not just a normal tin, a supersize one that they would use in catering or something. And he put the tin on the scales and he said loudly to everyone, 'See, the scales are a pound out! That tin should be 2 pounds and it's only 1 pound.'

And the inspector simply said, 'OK, go on then Jane, get on again, I got on again and I read 141lbs again but because Angelo had announced the scales were out by one pound, the inspector simply said, 'Angelo's right, you're 140lbs.'

So I was able to box and I didn't have to lose any extra weight simply because the reputation of this great man, the respect that he commanded, no one was going to argue with him! It was another insight into a world I was beginning to learn so much so rapidly about. It's not just the ten two-minute rounds that people watch on TV ... the politics behind it all is unreal!

That fight in New Orleans was an experience that I wanted to forget but wasn't going to be an isolated incident. I came down with pneumonia after the fight, I think from training so hard in the build-up and running on empty. And the problem was, Tex was always in the background, tempting me with the next fight, promising it would be different.

'I know you didn't get paid that time Jane but another trip has come up, fancy it?'

The carrot had been dangled in front of me again and yet I am the one getting battered each time. I am the one putting my heart and soul into every fight. I wanted it so much in Denmark I would have died that night for that title; I wanted it so much in New Orleans but I didn't get paid ... and then it's time for the next one and you go again and then again and then again. It's exhausting.

'One day it will all be worth it, next time it will be different,' he'd say. Before going for the knockout punch.

'Well, if you don't fight, someone else will, there is always another fighter who'll take your place.'

So I began to justify each fight. New Orleans ... OK, I didn't get paid but at least we got fed. It was one step up from Copenhagen. See how easy it is? See the way it just tightens its grip on you at every turn?

Of course, there were times when boxing brought me opportunities that I would never have normally had, so I will always be grateful to it for that. Always. Especially when, just after coming back from New Orleans, I went to the first-ever Pride of Britain Awards. This was a few years before they got going properly and it started becoming the annual, televised extravaganza it is now.

When we received a letter through at the farm inviting us to the awards I would like to say I was excited but these events normally mean dressing up and I didn't like that idea one fucking bit. Wearing a dress or dressing up is well out of my comfort zone, but Tex double-checked and it was definitely a formal occasion, so I went out and bought the most plain one I could. It was loose, black and floor-length and it was the best they were going to get. The awards were being held at the Dorchester Hotel in London. It was a really beautiful, swanky venue and we were all a bit stunned when we got there as there was a red carpet and lots of waiting paparazzi and press.

The awards celebrated ordinary people who had achieved extraordinary things and there were categories for bravery, for volunteering, for being pioneers. It felt like a real honour to have been invited. I was still so new to boxing, yet because I won the world title the year before I felt like this was a little nod of appreciation in my direction. And I felt proud. I had done something and perhaps I was being accepted a little. It was early afternoon when we arrived and the red carpet with the waiting press and photographers got very little attention from me. But I don't suppose they gave me a lot of attention either, the place was full of celebrities and famous people and some of them I knew, but others I didn't have a clue. I walked the red carpet as quickly as I could, I did have to stop and pose for a bit but a quick grin, a quick fist up and I was done. When I got inside I recognised a few folk from the telly but other than that it wasn't exactly filled with people that I would normally want to spend an afternoon with. But then again, I thought to myself, it could be fun. And it was a day out from training, from the farm.

When we went inside the hotel there was a real buzz to the proceedings, like something special was happening, and I succumbed to it; it wasn't long before I was caught up in the atmosphere too. 'I'm here, celebrating some amazing people and some amazing stories,' I thought, and I bloody deserve to enjoy myself and let my hair down. Tex and another friend of mine who'd come along with me all went through to the awards room and off to find our table. When we got there I immediately recognised one of the people sitting there, it was only bloody Jimmy Corkhill from *Brookie*! Of course, that was his character in the TV soap, Dean Sullivan was the actor's real name, although I think I called him Jimmy most of the night! I was totally star-struck to begin with, I loved *Brookside*, but he was such an easy-going, funny guy we started chatting and got on like a house on fire. He's a good bloke Dean, he was fun and we had the same sense of humour. Not to mention he was a bit of a mouthy scouser and I was a mouthy Lancashire bird so we had lots in common.

And I don't know at what point we realised, but all of a sudden we had a new guest at our table. And not just any new table buddy, royalty! Princess Diana had walked in and she had sat down at our table and probably for the first time in our lives Dean and I were completely speechless. I could not think of a single word to say. What would you say? Princess Diana had come in and was sitting right next to me and I was in complete shock. She sat down, completely at ease, smiled at us and said, 'Hello, nice to meet you.' I was still completely speechless and I heard Dean say, 'Nice to meet you ma'am,' so I quickly found my voice and said the same, 'Nice to meet you.'

It was one of the most surreal moments of my life. But she was so normal and down-to-earth that it wasn't long before we just sort of chatted and you would forget that she was a princess and had been married to the future king of England. To have that kind of skill of putting people at ease, she had such a charming, natural way about her. Dean was hilarious, he'd come out with, 'It's so lovely to see you Di, you're looking so well,' like they were old mates or something. But I guess that was because she was so polite and enchanting, you really did feel like you could tell her anything.

She asked me what I did as she didn't have a clue who I was and why would she? She's blimmin' royalty and I'm, well, I'm Jane.

And when I told her she just wanted to know everything about women boxing. She was fascinated that women were doing this, absolutely fascinated. I told her I felt exactly the same as her when I first saw it, I was captivated too when I had seen the documentary on Channel 4.

'But why weren't you in the documentary then?' she asked.

'It was filmed in America,' I said. 'It's illegal to box here.'

And I will never forget her wide-eyed reaction, she just said, 'Wow ... wow ...' She couldn't believe it but she was desperate to know more, she wanted to know everything about boxing.

We just sat there chatting and I told her all she wanted to know. She was asking lots of questions and then when I'd answer them, she'd go quiet for a little bit, like she was deep in thought, then she'd ask some more.

'So, you like to box then? Do you hit people in the face? When's the next fight Jane, is it in America? Will it be shown in England?'

And I'd tell her about my fights so far and what it's like in the ring and she'd listen, think about it and ask some more:

'Do you wear breast protection Jane?'

And I said, 'I ain't got any tits, Di!'

'Does it hurt when you get hit?'

'Of course it does!' I told her. 'It bloody hurts!'

Tom (left), me and Bozzy, the three musketeers.

My mum's boyfriend Lenny Smith and Bozzy (John Boswell), mine and Tom's best mate.

Having a good sparring session at the Farm with Luke Clayfield.

Me and Stu McKenzie, he was always in my corner and helping me train.

[and below]: 1997, Foxwood Studios, putting my heart and soul into fighting Leah Mellinger for the WIBF light welterweight belt.

Going into battle with the BBBC at court.

Proudly showing off my WIBF light welterweight title belt at the press conference after our historic legal win.

Legally allowed to box in the UK, I squared up to my opponent, Simona Lukic.

Winning my fight against Lukic, it was the first time I was a 'home' fighter and it was a fantastic night.

The press conference after the Lukic fight. It was a hugely successful occasion and I saw lots of women in the audience cheering.

At the David Lloyd Club in Raynes Park London, winning the WIBF light welterweight title.

Shaking hands with Lucia Rijker at the Staples Center in Los Angeles. She was the toughest female opponent I've faced.

Rijker burst my eardrum in the second round and I lost all my balance but kept giving her everything I had.

My fight with Rijker was on the undercard of the Vitali Klitschko (pictured) versus Lennox Lewis fight.

2006 match against Holly Holm in New Mexico, a year before I retired.

'Alright mate!' Receiving my MBE from Prince Charles in 2007.

With David Haye in London. He is a good, sound bloke.

With John Conteh, a former WBC light-heavyweight champion and Liverpudlian legend.

With the iconic American boxer, 'Sugar' Ray Leonard.

With Paul Speak and Ricky Hatton, two life-long friends.

Interviewing, and ...

... posing with Tyson Fury for a fundraising charity event.

Joe Calzaghe, Ricky Hatton and Gary Jacobs.

Me and Tom. The first famous Couch!

My wonderful, formidable, tough-as-nails mother.

'I'm Jane's Dad!' Dad would let everyone know I was his daughter when he came to my home fights.

Me and Brian with Frank Bruno, who I've known and been good friends with for years.

Meeting Brian after my breakdown. He is my rock and we've been together ever since I challenged him to find me in Bristol.

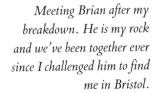

And there was so much laughter and fun and swearing and joking. She was just normal and fascinated by everything I was telling her, including all about the court case that we were bringing against the BBBC (British Boxing Board of Control) the following year.

'I've got a posh lawyer,' I said. 'I know posh people too!'

'What do you mean?' she asked.

'Well, you're like the queen,' I said.

'I'm not the queen!' she replied, very matter-of-factly.

'You know what I mean, Di,' I said, 'you're a princess and I'm a fighter. But my lawyer's posh though!'

And she thought it was hilarious.

'What were the arguments for women to not box then?' she said.

'Because women are unstable,' I said.

'They got that right!' she said, laughing. And we were all laughing by this time, absolutely laughing our heads off.

She was just so nice. Her interest in the boxing was brilliant. She was so genuinely interested because she had never heard of women boxing and I was telling her everything – anything she asked, I would tell her.

And how weird, nearly ten years later, I would be meeting Prince Charles at Buckingham Palace and we would get on so well too. Who knew I'd be so at ease with royalty?! I could slot right in that family I reckon!

She had security with her but you wouldn't know they were there, they all sort of mingled in and she was able to relax a bit. I think one of them sat at the table with us as we didn't have many people at our table – there were probably only about seven people, me and Tex, Dean, Diana, one of her security team and an athlete I think. And it wasn't just a quick, flying visit to each table. She sat at our table for the whole dinner chatting with us until she was called up on to stage to do her speech. We ate a three-course meal together and I tried to impress her with my knowledge of using the right cutlery for the right course – I thought it was impressing her but of course it completely backfired.

The first course was soup and when it was brought out and put in front of us, I turned to her and said, 'It's the outside fork you know Di, outside in.' And I had the biggest, cheekiest grin on my face.

And she was crying with laughter and simply replied, 'Yes Jane, unless you're having soup and then it's the spoon!'

And we both started to laugh. And giggling, well, who better would I want to share a joke with than that wonderful woman?

She kept the conversation flowing with everyone on the table but as I was next to her, literally within touching distance, quite often we'd be in our own little world.

'Jane, is your hair natural? It's really curly isn't it?'

I had it down this afternoon, it's normally tied right back for a fight so when it is down and left to its natural curly devices, it's quite impressive I suppose. Even to a princess!

And equally, I just couldn't stop staring at this beautiful woman who was sitting next to me. She was just so mesmerising and her skin was just glowing, it was perfect, like a porcelain doll, and I couldn't help but stare at her. 'I can't believe I am sitting next to Princess Diana,' I'd be saying in my head, 'this is fucking amazing.'

Can you imagine if it happened now? Oh I'd be tweeting from the table that's for sure: 'Hello Twitterverse, me and Di here, just chatting about boxing and having lunch, as you do!'

The awards themselves were brilliant because they were celebrating everyday folk doing amazing things and for Princess Diana to be there helped make them realise how special they were. She had that effect on you, she'd make you feel special. The room was full of other celebrities too and I know they were all completely at ease with the red-carpet experience and being photographed, whereas the woman next to me was fed up with it all, she was sick of being hounded by the press. You couldn't pick up a newspaper or a magazine and not see photos of her on the front cover. She was always on the TV being followed by all these cameras and photographers as she just tried to go to the gym.

And she told us all about it. She told us how unbearable and relentless it was. And the way she was talking, you could see the pain on her face and the fact she knew she couldn't do anything about it, it wasn't going to get any better, because of who she was. The way she was chatting to me and Dean … it was like she was offloading and it was like she needed to vent a little I guess.

'I'd tell 'em all to fuck off,' I said to her, like I was just chatting to a mate. She was so friendly and normal that even swearing seemed normal because she was just so lovely. Look, you'll have to cut me some slack, I was star-struck when I first got to the table and realised I was sitting with Jimmy Corkhill from *Brookie* let alone when Princess Di sits next to me!

When she left the table to go up to do her speech and present a big award at the end of the dinner, we were all a little heartbroken that she was leaving us. No one wanted the afternoon to end! And after she had been telling us about the press, Dean shouted over to her, in his thick scouse accent just as she approached the stage, 'Aye Di, don't let the bastards get you down!' I was crying with laughter and she looked back at us with a big smile on her face and it was just magical, there is no other word to describe it.

Now, you can take me out of Fleetwood but it seemed you couldn't take the Fleetwood out of me and when I went to the toilets I had no idea about toilet attendants. Not a clue. So you can imagine my surprise when I came out of the toilet and this woman came straight over to me and started to brush my dress down with a clothes brush. 'Whoa!' I said, 'What the fuck are you doing?! Get away from me!'

I had no idea who she was until another lady in the toilets explained it to me and calmed down the situation. The poor toilet attendant, I think I must have scared her with my reaction but I was equally shocked! And you're meant to tip them too? I had no clue about any of this, it's not like I've been in many posh toilets in my life, is it? I was so embarrassed but my first thought when I came out and went back to the table was that I'll have to tell Di what's happened. 'She'll love that story,' I thought. But by the time I went back to the table I couldn't see her anywhere, the awards were finished and I assumed she must have made her getaway already. I sat back down and started to recount the story to Dean when I sensed movement through the room and I turned to see she was being whisked away. And then, across two tables, as she carried on walking with her security team, she called over to me, 'Jane!' And I waved and shouted back, 'Di! I'll catch you soon, yeah?!'

And she put two thumbs up. That is a memory I will cherish for as long as I live.

I was in Paris when I found out she had died, how fucking weird is that. I wasn't in France to fight, I can't remember why I was there, just that the whole city was alight with this raw sense of tragedy. It was less than a year since I had seen her and I made a note then and there to mentally lock in that memory of our afternoon together. I never wanted to forget it.

When I switched on the TV at the hotel you could see there had been an accident involving her and her boyfriend Dodi Fayed as their photos were up on screen but I didn't understand a word of what was being said. It was only when I found a BBC channel that it became clear, a car accident ... fatalities ... and I sat there completely stunned. I felt so honoured to have met her, I still feel so honoured to have met her, that won't ever change. And the funny thing is, she'll never realise what a boost it gave me, spending the afternoon, eating lunch and chatting away to her. I went straight back to the farm after the awards were finished and instead of the usual dread, I felt so positive. I went back to training with a new sense of purpose, of motivation, all because of her. Cheers for that Di. Cheers from the bottom of my heart.

* * *

Five months after my New Orleans fight I was back in the ring in Connecticut. I was due to fight a boxer called Leah Mellinger to retain my title again. This was a pretty massive fight for me and one hell of a night overall – Roy Jones Jr topped the bill boxing Montell Griffin that same evening. That was a huge fight and to be the undercard fighter for the likes of Roy Jones Jr, who was a big name in America and all over the world, made me refocus on the night ahead. Our fight was the opening fight, the women's show at the start of the evening, but still with an ABC TV network filming the whole evening, the viewing figures were in their tens of millions. It was on such a huge scale. We flew in and went pretty much straight to the weigh-in. It was a bit more of a glamorous affair this time, it was held inside a large cinema complex inside the Foxwood Casino, one of the biggest casinos in the world where some of the biggest fights in history have taken place. It was just jaw-dropping, I had never seen anything so massive in all my life. You'd be lost in that place for days easily!

When you fight in America, everything is just on a huge basis, the scale of the shows they put on, the scale of the venues, everything was just massive. I pinched myself a good few times, Foxwoods was a world away from Fleetwood!

It didn't occur to me then that there'd be a problem with any aspect of my trip that night – other than losing to Leah, which hadn't even crossed my mind to be honest – since we hadn't been fed or paid the previous two international fights, what else could go wrong? I was fighting the same night as these two pound-for-pound boxing legends in a televised event that would be shown around the world. This wasn't the big time, that would only come in my mind when I could fight in my own country, but it pretty damn close. So when we went to check in to our room the day before the fight and discovered there was just one room and four of us, I guess I was surprised but not that surprised. Does that make sense? It was like they wanted you to be part of something remarkable, a moment of history, part of the fight of the year, but at the same time they didn't really want you. I was of use, they knew my fights were tough, gritty and entertaining to watch. I got the crowds roaring and fired up before the main event but I didn't quite deserve the full world-champion treatment. I was still female after all.

So the night before my big fight I found myself sleeping on one of the recliners in the middle of the casino, propped up against one of the fruit machines. The recliners are for the all-night gamblers, the ones who don't ever want to admit defeat. Casinos aren't stupid, they won't display clocks or have windows, just that bright, unchanging light so no one knows the time of day or how long you've been gambling away your life. Sleeping down here was the last option. We had tried to buy a room at the hotel but they were all sold out because of the fight.

'I'm fighting!' I screamed in my head, 'where am I going to sleep?!'

I started chatting to one of the cleaners who told me about a motel down the road. Only it turned out to be over 60 miles away and I then had to explain to her that was too far as I was due back here for my fight tomorrow.

But I've slept in worse places and there really was no point fucking fussing, I had a job to do the next day and I wanted to get whatever rest I could.

My fight didn't get off to the best start, I was knocked back by a right punch and staggered a few steps back, a little shocked by the venom from this otherwise glamorous-looking opponent. She had a cover-girl look about her and was overly made-up but she was tough and she was strong. That staggering punch made me refocus on the job at hand so I was able to start doing what I do best, relentlessly battling and battling. We went the full ten rounds that night, the audience there roaring and cheering and loud in their appreciation of a good boxing match. I was buzzing too, I was announced the winner on points and although it was a tough slog, I didn't feel, apart from the blip in the first round, that I had lost control.

George Foreman, the ex-world heavyweight champion was watching the fight and gave me one of his badges. He told Tex that 'he had a good girl there.'

And also in the audience was Hollywood actor Denzel Washington. I saw him staring at me after the fight and I couldn't work out why. Did he want to talk to me? He did come over in the end and simply said, 'Good fight, very good fight.'

'Yeah, it was wasn't it?!' I was pretty full of adrenaline still and on a high from winning. Hollywood actor or no Hollywood actor, I was buzzing and I was pleased Denzel, who is a massive boxing fan, approved!

If the boxing world treated me as basically as they could, to the American public I was like royalty! Because the fight had been shown on TV and the audience viewing figures were in their millions, I was a familiar face when we got back to the airport for the flight home. Lots of people wanted to come up and say hello, to tell me they'd watched my fight, to say well done to me. It was amazing, I did feel like a bit of a rock star and always waved or grinned like the cat who'd got the cream – and retained the world title. I think I got paid around $500 – not forgetting an extra $500 later from Barry for that experience. Again, once everything had been paid there wasn't a lot left to line my pockets so I wasn't exactly living a rock star lifestyle.

I did think about moving to America several times after those fights. I was allowed to box legally in that country, I was recognised and not thought of as a freak or crazy. There was respect there.

But if I had stayed in America, well, I wouldn't have made a difference would I? Because while I was kipping on the floor of the biggest casino in the world and getting stared at by Hollywood film stars, there were two brilliant legal minds putting together a case to take the British Board of Boxing Control to court so I could box, legally, as a woman, in England.

Chapter Six

Taking the devil to court

*'For future female British boxing
champions, indeed, all women who
choose to box, Jane's name is set to
acquire all the resonance of the most
prominent suffragettes.'*

Irish Times

IF there is a date I will never forget, that is etched in my
memory forever and won't ever lose its significance, I
would say that Monday, 30 March 1998 is it. It's not
just a date that means something to me either, it's a date
that, factually speaking, changed the course of history. I
think about that date now and wonder how different life
would be, how this juggernaut of an event, which took place
in a small courtroom in south London, not only changed

my life but the lives of hundreds of sportswomen in the years to come.

And the funny thing is, I hadn't planned to be part of it. I was someone who was just trying to earn a living through boxing and was frustrated that this was something I couldn't do in this country. After my fight in New Orleans I was taking part in the usual press conference when I said something that was to cause an equal rights solicitor to prick up her ears. I hadn't got paid, I was cross. If I was a British male boxer in America I would have support, I would be covered by the British Boxing Board of Control who would look after me. But I was a woman, I had no back-up, I had no licence, no one was going to help me.

Tex had just told me that I had been offered a big money fight in Wembley. I'd been knocked for six. Here I was, just lost out on payment in America, and now I had to turn down a ten-grand fight in my own country as I wasn't legally allowed to box in England.

I was mad, and during that interview my frustration showed.

'I want to fight in my own country, I've been offered a fight at Wembley for £10k but the bastards won't let me box cos they won't give me a licence,' I ranted to journalists. It wasn't tactful but it was the truth. I didn't care by then. I honestly didn't expect anything to come from it. And then I had a phone call that was going to change my life.

Sara Leslie, a pioneering solicitor in the area of discrimination law and equal pay, wasn't someone I was ever likely to meet in my entire life if I hadn't said those angry words at that press conference. And yet she was someone who has changed my entire life too.

She wanted to know a bit more about me, what I had been doing and who I had been fighting and where. She wanted to know about the title I had won and retained. And lastly, she wanted to know exactly why I couldn't fight at Wembley and earn £10,000. She had no knowledge of the boxing world, no idea who was in charge of what or sanctioned what, so I simply explained that to box legally and professionally in this country, every boxer needed a licence from the British Boxing Board of Control, BBBC. I couldn't get this licence because they didn't grant them to women.

She listened to all I had to say and then said simply, 'Jane, that's wrong, they can't do that.'

'They can, it's the law. It's illegal for me to box here.' Even as I was saying it, it wasn't registering, it was just something that I had come to accept, a law that was in place long before I started to box.

'No, Jane, they can't do it.' Sara was insistent and very matter-of-fact. Obviously I knew it was unfair and a pain in the arse, but until that point it was just that. I just accepted it at the time, it was what it was. I had no intention of being a big pioneer for the sport, to make a stand for women boxers in the UK, I was just interested in making a living.

But what Sara was telling me made sense. I wasn't being allowed to earn a living in my own country and that was wrong.

'You're very good at your job, you've proved you are good at what you do,' she said. 'It's not like you've just started boxing, you're a world champion and you have defended your title, and you are being stopped from doing your job in this country. That is restriction of trade.'

I sat in silence as she continued: 'If you were just a one-fight novice I couldn't defend you but you are an established fighter. You can fight all over the world but not in this country. It's not right and I want to take on your case.'

It was one of those moments when my life changed forever. Sara came up to Bristol from London after that and explained what would be happening. She talked me through everything that she was planning and that she had been in contact with Dinah Rose, a QC, who would be working on our case and who would be representing me when we took the BBBC to court.

The first thing that Sara wanted me to do was prove that I couldn't indeed get a licence because I was female. I needed to show that although I met every other criteria for being able to box legally in this country, I wouldn't be granted a licence because I wasn't a man.

So I did, I applied for a licence. I filled out an application form knowing it would be turned down, but it didn't matter, we then had the paperwork to show for it.

Once you submit your application you have to go in front of the board for an interview and I had to travel to somewhere near Cornwall to complete this process.

I walked into the room, which was full of ex-trainers, ex-managers and ex-fighters who all sat on the board.

'What are you doing here?' was the first question, to which I gave an obvious reply.

'I've come to apply for a professional boxing licence.'

And they interviewed me as they would interview a male boxer. I answered all their questions, I told them I had passed all the medical tests, the brain scan, the blood tests. We went through everything that I would go through if I was a male boxer.

They let me get through all of this before they turned around and said, 'Sorry, we can't license you because you're a woman.'

And that was that. There was an older guy on the board, I can't remember his name, and as I was walking out of the room he just shouted over to me, 'Why the fuck do you want to box? You're just wasting everybody's time.'

So I just turned around and said, 'OK, I'll see you in court.'

'It won't even make court,' he sneered.

I left the room, his words ringing in my ears, and rang Sara. I told her my licence had been denied and she simply said, 'Great, get me all the paperwork,' and that was that.

She knew that was going to happen but all the board had done was give her more fuel for the fire.

Sara Leslie then introduced me to Dinah, who was to be our barrister. She had been at the Bar for about six years or something like that and had worked with Sara on a number of other discrimination cases, including the case about women working in a banknote-printing factory who had been paid less than the male workers.

Sara contacted Dinah about my case and when I met her she told me she had just had a baby and come back from maternity leave. She said that when my case had come across her desk she thought it was amazing. And from that point on I knew I was in safe hands. Sara and Dinah were so passionate and so supportive and when we had our first meeting, I felt for the first time in my life someone cared. Someone actually agreed with what I wanted to do and they wanted to help me do it. They told me that they had issued the claim against the BBBC for their refusal to grant me a licence on what they called 'medical grounds', and they talked me through how they would rip this defence to pieces.

I was 29 years old and we were putting our case to the courts at the beginning of 1998 – 1998, not 1898. And when Dinah told me of the defence, what they actually stated as their case for why they wouldn't grant me a licence, it was just unbelievable. The defence stated: 'Women are emotionally labile because they menstruate.'

Labile is a medical term meaning unstable. That was their defence. And the thing was, Sara and Dinah had put this case forward as a 'restriction of trade'. Their argument was that I should be able to just get on with my job, I'm world champion, I'm good at what I do, let me work. We didn't set out to expose them for being sexist, they did that themselves with their defence, we wanted it recognised as a simple fact that I wasn't allowed to do it as a trade and that was unfair. We weren't ever saying this is everyone's trade and certainly not everyone will want to box. But I did, and they were stopping me from earning a living.

I had told Mum what was happening, but she didn't come down for the court case. In the end it went on longer than we were expecting and I ended up staying at a B&B in Croydon while it was going on. All three of us were just so focused on winning and getting the licence, it was all-encompassing. And the funny thing is, I didn't go out to upset the BBBC, I wasn't out to set the world alight. If they had said to me, 'We'll give you a licence if you drop everything and go away quietly,' I would have said yes! Of course I would have done. I even gave them that option in the beginning. I remember saying to them, 'Forget the case, just give me a licence', but back then they were so adamant they were going to win, they were so convinced that no court would ever disagree with them. And Dinah and Sara, having seen their defence, were never going to let this settle for anything other than a court case. When the option did come up, quite close to the tribunal, and they contacted us to ask if we'd settle out of court, I was still all for it. But Dinah and Sara knew this went far bigger than just me. 'You should have your day in court,' they said. 'They should be exposed for who they are.'

And Dinah said something to me I will never forget: 'You have a 100 per cent chance of success,' she said. And 20 years later she told me that this is still the only time she has ever said that to a client.

'If we don't win I will eat my wig,' she said. And in that moment, I had never felt so powerful.

The court case began in February and there was already quite a lot of press interest and media attention on it. The fact that I, a woman, was taking a huge, historic, boxing establishment to court for the right to box was big news. But what was to become bigger news, as Sara, Dinah, and I already knew, was the defence the BBBC were putting up. It made headlines, quite rightly, for its stupidity and ignorance and blatant disregard of the truth.

A solicitor representing the board, Bernard Buckley, laid out his client's case in front of the three tribunal judges, one of whom was a woman. He made it clear that their defence, and their entire defence, was built on the assumption that 'many women suffer from premenstrual tension which makes them emotional and more labile and accident-prone. They are too fragile to box and they bruise easily. They also might be unknowingly in the early stages of pregnancy and they might be prone to breast cancer due to being punched in the chest repeatedly.' They also said that all contraceptives and painkillers taken for period pains would not be allowed.

They called in Dr Adrian Whiteson, a medical advisor for the BBBC, to back up their case. There was no holding Dinah back at this point, it was like watching a lion getting ready to go in for the kill. Every single line of their defence was going to be shot to pieces because it was completely untrue and it was just a case of watching Dinah toying with her prey for a few minutes before going for the jugular.

'So, if women are more emotionally unstable, you wouldn't want a woman in any kind of responsible job presumably,' she said.

'No, I'd be very concerned.'

'So, piloting a plane?' She continued. 'You probably wouldn't want a woman to do anything like that?'

'No, I don't think so,' he said.

'Or leave a woman in charge of small children? That would obviously be very dangerous and probably be quite a bad idea then?'

'Yes, yes, yes.'

And the whole court just erupted at the ludicrousness of it. The journalists in the room were laughing their heads off and even the female judge shook her head. The doctor didn't say anything. But Dinah wasn't finished.

'Do you have any evidence to suggest Jane has periods?'

'All women have periods. She shouldn't be boxing when she's on her period,' he said.

'But how do you know Jane Couch has periods?'

'Because she's a woman,' he said.

'Well actually,' continued Dinah, 'athletes don't always have periods and she is an athlete. When their bodies are in training and when they lose a certain amount of body fat they don't bleed.'

Some of the answers to Dinah's questions had made it into the media circus this was fast becoming. Dinah was proving every part of their argument was false and she wasn't finished. It was my turn now, I was ready to do my bit.

'Jane, you have been refused a licence to box in this country by the BBBC, why do you think this is?'

'I was informed that my application was refused on medical grounds. But I maintain that the application was refused on sex discrimination grounds. I do not suffer from premenstrual tension or painful periods. I have a pregnancy test before every bout so pregnancy cannot be a reason.' Another part of their defence had been smashed to pieces and it felt good.

Dinah was on a roll and every journalist was hanging on her every word.

'The BBBC are trying to protect boxing as the last male bastion of sport against the participation of women,' she began.

'It's like when they told women they couldn't run marathons because their wombs would fall out. It's the most disgraceful stereotyping of women and I struggle to think of a more audacious or outrageous plea in a sexual discrimination case in the last ten years. Jane is currently the welterweight champion of the world. However, although she is a British boxer, all of her title fights have to be held abroad because the BBBC have refused to give her a professional licence. In effect, she is wholly shut out from professional boxing in this country.'

Over the past few days we had shown the BBBC for what they really were and the case hadn't concluded yet. The newspapers were reporting heavily on the PMT angle and 'women being too fragile to box', which was great – the whole country was beginning to see how archaic and sexist the board were and there was absolutely no coming back from it for them.

But they wouldn't give up. They called Leonard Read, president and chairman of the board, to give his views. His name might not sound familiar but he was mostly known as 'Nipper' Read in those days. He was the detective who sent the notorious Kray twins to prison. A well-respected, intelligent, well-known policeman with a celebrated history of bringing two of the most hardened criminals in this country to justice. And what a fall from the pedestal he took when he stood up in court and tried to justify the board's decision. As the defence had not given me a licence on medical grounds, Dinah asked him if I had been medically examined before my application was rejected.

'No,' he said.

'So why then?'

'Women's boxing will only attract alleged fans who want to see women fighting as much as they do women's mud wrestling,' he said. 'The problem with women fighting is that you get the brown-mac brigade all watching.'

Dinah, Sara and I could honestly not believe what we were hearing, the absolute stupidity of it all. The BBBC obviously thought that by bringing out the big guns, the chairman, a man as well respected as Nipper Read, there would be a lot of weight to his argument. The judges would listen to him. But in the end it backfired spectacularly and I think it was after his testimony that they threw the case out of court. When the tribunal judges said there was no case, it was the best feeling in the world. Dinah had told me right at the beginning that there was no way that any tribunal who heard my case will not find in my favour, and she was right.

It meant so much to me, so much to all three of us, it was like we had become such a close team that even though this decision would change my life, it was also going to have a profound effect on them as well. It felt like it was us against them and we had won and now the law was going to change thanks to Dinah and Sara.

'Jane Couch has been extremely badly treated by the boxing board,' they said. 'She has suffered incontrovertible sexual discrimination and there is overwhelming evidence that her request for a licence was turned down because she is female. The medical grounds on which her licence was rejected were all gender-based stereotypes and assumptions.' They gave the BBBC 42 days to settle the matter.

I was absolutely jubilant, I felt like I could take on the world with Sara and Dinah, and in a way we had. We had made history, and although I was doing this for myself, for my right to earn a living in my country, I knew then the implication of this court case. Now if any other women can meet the strict criteria of being able to box, their application can't be rejected simply because they are female.

Coming out of court, we were met with a huge media circus. I couldn't keep the smile off my face, I was beaming and I was trying to look in every direction as my name was shouted by the photographers. I had no media training, no advice about how to handle what was happening, but at that moment I didn't care. The whole street outside the court was lit up with cameras flashing and there was a lot of shouting and I probably looked a lot like a rabbit in headlights at that point. I was nervous, I couldn't express myself very well, and I think I kept repeating how pleased I was and how excited I was to finally be able to box in this country.

The press conference following the court case was as equally packed and energetic, and with Sara and Dinah by my side I felt completely ready to face questions. I wasn't prepared for the media backlash, however. I didn't appreciate what a huge event this was in the world of sport, to me it was just a case of being able to earn a living in my country. To some media commentators, however, what I had done was 'disgusting' and women boxing was only ever going to be a 'freak show'. A *Daily Mail* reporter wrote that Sara, Dinah and I looked like 'lesbians' at the press conference, as if that was a massive insult, and of course only butch, gay women would want women to box. How could they get away with that? I was so upset for Dinah and Sara when I read that, I was fuming and I felt this personal attack was all my fault. But they completely laughed it off. They had been called a lot worse they said, they didn't care.

Dinah did care about me, however, and after that press conference she pulled me aside: 'Your fight is only just beginning,' she told me. And in my ignorance, I had no idea what she meant.

NOTES FROM MY LAWYER, DINAH ROSE QC:

The first time I met Jane she just seemed to glow. She was the healthiest looking person I have ever seen. She was obviously incredibly physically fit and she looked amazing. She is a very charismatic, larger-than-life character and as soon as I met her I was impressed with her enthusiasm, her vibrancy and her dedication to her sport.

The tribunal hearing took two or three days but I know Sara had been in contact with Jane for several months leading up to this moment. The hearing itself was very intense. Jane gave evidence and the defence had two or three witnesses on their behalf. There was a doctor and a witness from the board who was a retired policeman who had been involved in hunting down the Kray twins.

One of the Board's defences was the remarkable claim that women are emotionally unstable because of their menstrual cycle, and that they therefore could not safely be licenced to box. This amounted to saying, in effect, that all women are more unstable than Mike Tyson, since the Board had been prepared to licence him even after he had bitten off part of Evander Holyfield's ear. The Board called a doctor to support this part of their defence. He gave evidence under cross examination that women could not safely be permitted to perform any responsible job, and that they should not even be left alone in charge of small children.

The Board also sought to argue that women could not be licensed because, under the rules, professional boxers were required to be stripped to the waist.

I said to them, 'You know, it's not too hard to get around that is it? I mean, women could wear a vest couldn't they? Does it just come down to the vest?'

'Yes' came the answer from the Board's witness. 'Yes, it just comes down to a vest.'

The Board's defence was just ridiculous. People were openly laughing in the tribunal.

There was lots of press coverage and that press coverage was very polarised. There were a lot of people who were very strongly opposed to women boxing. They thought it was disgusting, a horrible spectacle, and that it was indecent to allow women to fight in public. There was a lot of stuff written with a lot of venom, and some of it was quite personally abusive towards Sara and me. But we won, as we knew we would.

I have often wondered why the Board were so convinced they would win with such flimsy, outrageously sexist defence. I think there are two likely possibilities, though I am only speculating. One is that the Board wasn't actually that keen to win the case. Sometimes you get a situation where the defendant feels they have to defend the position, regardless of its merit, because it might be politically impossible to do anything else. They might have thought their membership wouldn't accept it if they simply just changed the rules when Jane came in for a licence, so they might have had to put up a little bit of a fight. I don't know, that is just a possibility. The other possibility is that they didn't fully understand the law. The barrister who represented them was somebody involved in boxing but who didn't have a track record as a discrimination lawyer. So in effect, they may not have known what they were doing given how specialised this field is.

But I am speculating, I don't know the truth of the matter but I do know that their case wasn't very impressive.

I think one of the lessons you learn from doing cases like this is that the law can only take you so far, and in the real world, whatever your legal rights are, that is just part of the battle. I said to Jane, after we had won the case, I wasn't sure if her battle to box was actually won.

You look at women who have been pioneers in all kinds of fields, they have had to sacrifice so much in order for the future generations to succeed. In my own field, there was a woman in the early 20th century called Gwyneth Bebb who wanted to be a lawyer. She took the law final exams at Cambridge and got the equivalent of a First Class degree but they wouldn't give it to her because she was a woman. She wanted to be a solicitor but they wouldn't let her be one so she took the Law Society to court. The Court of Appeal ruled that she couldn't be a solicitor because the word 'person' in the Solicitors Act didn't include women. Women were not 'persons' apparently. In 1919 they passed the Sex Disqualification Removal Act so that women were allowed to become Solicitors and Barristers. Gwyneth Bebb qualified to be a barrister, but before she could start practising she died from complications in childbirth.

To me, that story is both tragic and inspiring, and epitomises the struggle that women have faced in many fields. Gwyneth Bebb was socially and academically excluded, then she was legally and professionally excluded, and she had to overcome all of those barriers, which she did. Then she was defeated by the risks of childbirth. It's really hard. I think we should be incredibly grateful to the women who have come before us and broken the ground. I don't think we think about it enough.

I have huge respect for Jane and what she did. She took on a hugely powerful establishment at enormous emotional cost. She had a big impact in my life. I have done lots of high-profile cases over the years but hers is definitely in my top five.

And there is an important postscript to Jane's case. In 2012 women's boxing was an Olympic sport and Nicola Adams won a gold medal for the UK. It was amazing and moving to see how the whole country got behind her. Everyone just accepted her boxing as a legitimate sport. It was one of those moments when you can see social attitudes change almost overnight. It was fantastic. I remember Nicola Adams gave interviews after that fight where she credited Jane as the pioneer of women's boxing. I think that was a lovely and fitting thing for her to do, and that she was right.'

Chapter Seven

Winning the battle but losing the war

'None but a vicarious pervert would pay to see two women belting the breasts off one another.'

Ian Wooldridge, *Daily Mail* sports writer,
1 April 1998

W HEN I first started to box, I was mixing with all the great fighters you've ever read about, I was boxing abroad, training at the farm, meeting people and telling a few journalists how great it would be if I could box legally in my country. And everything was quite exciting and positive and I guess I was happy in my bubble. I wasn't doing anyone any harm.

And then? Then, the tribunal court found the BBBC guilty of not giving me a boxing licence on sex discrimination grounds and my world turned upside down, quite literally overnight.

Instead of being just a female boxer wanting to earn a living through boxing, I was a monster who wanted all women in this country to fight.

The press were brutal, negative and vicious. It seemed that everything that was reported was biased in the BBBC's favour. The board appealed the decision, they were still convinced that the court was wrong and I was wrong and they were buoyed up by the reports calling me, Sara and Dinah lesbians, and me a freak and a monster. The appeal was denied, but it didn't matter, they had the press on their side. The press, the media and general public were against me. I thought I would just be allowed to get on with what I wanted to do, just get on and box, to continue to train and get on with my life, but the whole world wanted a piece of me. I was now the poster girl for all that was wrong with women's boxing. I was the villain, and I had no one standing up saying actually all she has done is won the right to earn a living the way she wants to.

And what got me the most were the personal attacks. The articles that were all just vicious assaults about the sort of person I was. The hurtful, unkind, derogatory stories about me and my life. They all slowly chip, chip, chipped away at me.

The problem was, everyone seemed to have an opinion, and that's OK, everyone is entitled to their own opinion, but when they know nothing about me or boxing it isn't really fair that they are vocal on things they know nothing about. People have said to me now, so many times, why didn't I say anything? Why didn't I complain about this treatment or why didn't I defend myself against this press? But I couldn't because I was part of it and I started playing up to it. Of course I regretted saying a lot of the things I did, a lot of the things I said. I'd spend hours crying afterwards, wondering why did I do this, why did I do that? And then I'd say to myself, 'Cheer up Jane! It's just one of those things, you've got your licence, who cares what people think?' And the next day I'd feel better again and I'd tell myself to get on with it.

After we came out of court victorious and the world's press were waiting outside for me, that moment of jubilation was just that – a short, fleeting moment. I didn't leave London for nearly four weeks, I was being taken from interview to interview, radio station to TV station to hotels for more press. I didn't know what I was doing, I was just being taken here there and everywhere, I was doing newspaper interviews in the morning then to a TV studio to do all sorts then back to radio for the afternoon. Tex had orchestrated it all, everyone wanted a piece of me, a piece of history I suppose, but I wasn't getting paid for any of it, I was just a puppet on a string, transported to different audiences, let out of a box and told to perform. And that was that. I just had to get on with it. But there was never a positive to that type of press, everyone just wanted to take the piss. I think I made such a point in the beginning by trying to sound upbeat and positive. 'In a few years' time, young girls will be able to go to their mums and say they want to be a boxer and they will be able to do it,' I told an interviewer for *The Independent*. 'And I don't think there's anything wrong in that.' I was clear with everyone at first that I knew I would still need to get my licence from the BBBC, but at least it wouldn't be refused because I was female. 'I work hard as a boxer and it will be nice to do it here,' I told the BBC. 'Women have my example to aim for and meet to set the standard. The boxing criteria of the boxing board is very, very strict. They have a strict medical and high standard. If women can't meet it, just like if a man can't meet it, they will not get a professional licence. But if they meet the standard and pass the medical then they should go ahead and box. That's what it's all about.' But every time I did an interview I felt like I was being set up. They didn't want me, they wanted this big bad monster that didn't exist.

Tex just wanted me to do everything and anything. I guess the exposure – good or bad – was good for him and his gym, and he didn't advise me not to enter into arguments but I didn't think I had a choice. I wasn't the sort of person to not defend myself so when the digs started

I would fight back, of course I would. They just wanted me to play that bad-girl character, the one who is making women box! No I'm not, I just want to get on with my job.

It wasn't a good experience, constantly being attacked, constantly being provoked. Every TV interview I took part in, they asked if I would wear my boxing clothes. They weren't interested in Jane the person, they wanted the Fleetwood Assassin, the character. Every time they asked I would try to say that I would prefer to just be in my normal clothes but that didn't work for them. They wanted this big bad character that didn't exist. If a male boxer has an interview, they don't make him dress up in his shorts and boxing gloves do they? Yes I had a rough upbringing but did they need to report about my fights and teenage years every time a story was written? It was wild, I have explained that, but it wasn't as bad as it was being reported. The press just seemed to focus on some tiny details, like my fights at school, and it makes me out to be a monster that I'm not. But when they start sowing a seed and giving you a reputation, you kind of just go along with it. I did. I thought it was easier, I didn't have the energy to fight it anymore. It was less exhausting to act the way they wanted and give them what they wanted. I don't know what I was thinking at the time but I think I believed that if they wanted to see this 'monster' so much, rather than a person who just had a dream, then that's what I should give them. Give the public what they want, isn't that what they say?

I had no media training, no advice and I couldn't express myself very well so it was much easier to fall into character.

Because of my northern accent I was immediately 'common' and 'classless'. Because I didn't go round in a dress, wasn't softly spoken and didn't have parents from a rich background, I was a chav. I see other girls coming into boxing now and I wonder why they are on the front cover of GQ magazine in their underwear. I couldn't do that, I didn't go into boxing to strip off, I went into boxing because I'm a fighter, I'm a world champion, I'm a hard woman, I'm not a girl pretending to box, I'm doing this to make a life for myself, to make a living because it's all I've got. It's all I can do, I have no education, I've got nothing. I just wanted to fight, I didn't know anything else.

I went on Michael Barrymore's show, *Barrymore*, which was a memorable event for all the wrong reasons. Michael was a huge household name in the 90s and his TV chat show was one of the biggest on the telly at the time. He would regularly get over 10 million viewers and I was asked to appear as he wanted to have a joke fight with me. No, I am not joking! I probably get recognised on the street more as being the woman who knocked out Barrymore than I do for my boxing career. What does that tell you?

Barrymore had asked me on to have a 'toy fight' with him in front of the studio audience. I remember chatting to Barbara Windsor in the green room beforehand and we were having a right laugh. I was excited but nervous as I wasn't really sure what he wanted me to do, but then his wife came in and explained more. I didn't get to meet Barrymore before the show, just his wife, who said that when it was my turn to go out, Michael would hold up some boxing pads for me to punch for a while then we'd do a little toy fight, it would all be a bit of fun and that would be that. The studio audience and viewers at home would love it she said, it's just a bit of fun. So I went out and he started off the play fight and then he kicked me! So I went for a light punch to his ribs and he went down, just like that, he fell on to the sofa. Then he called his security out of the audience to get me and I thought this was still part of the act so started sparring with them. It was honestly all done in jest and the audience were in fits of laughter, there was no maliciousness, no extreme or shock violence, I just did what I thought he wanted me to do. But because it was live TV, the way he acted when I hit him in the ribs made me look like a psycho! And the next day, on the front page of the *Daily Star*, there was a big photo of him getting into an ambulance with blood coming out of his ear!

Their headline was something like 'Fearsome boxer breaks Barrymore's ribs' or something like that. I was portrayed as a bully, a vicious animal and yet it was me who was asked to join in a joke fight with Barrymore in the name of entertainment! I'm not malicious. I'm not dangerous! I think the blood came from his earpiece, which must have come out either when I hit him or when he landed on the sofa.

My mum rang me and said, 'What have you done to Michael Barrymore?!'

'What? What are you on about Mum?'

'There are photos of him with blood running down his ear,' she said. It's on the front of the papers.

'That's where his ear piece came out when I hit him,' I said, 'he wanted me to fight him Mum!'

'And the broken rib?' she said.

'Ahhh, they're exaggerating,' I said. 'I lightly punched him and he was all dramatic cos he wanted the audience to laugh,' which they did. You could have asked anyone in the audience that day and they would have said the same, it was supposed to be a bit of fun.

After that he won a National Television Award and they showed clips of me on his show! It seemed like every interview or TV show or radio interview I did, everyone had their own agenda, but I couldn't see it at the time.

And the number of people who came up to me after the interview was incredible. I was an overnight household name but for all the wrong reasons – because I'd beaten up a national treasure! That world is just so false. The TV interviews got bigger and more frequent after that. I was either on it or being asked to be on it. *The Big Breakfast* was another massive show back then and there was a segment in which Vanessa Feltz would interview celebrity guests on a bed. I agreed to do it, and I took part when asked but again I wish I had someone telling me not to. It was early in the morning and I wasn't feeling particularly comfortable but I lay on the bed next to Vanessa. *The Big Breakfast* is completely live, which I did know so in the back of my mind I didn't think anything too bad would happen. But then as soon as we were told we were 'live', Vanessa launched her attack. 'I think it's disgusting,' she said. 'I think it's absolutely disgusting you punching women in the face.'

And I just looked at her, completely stunned by this attack.

'It's a sport,' I said, once I had composed myself. 'It's not just about punching women in the face.'

But she wouldn't give up. She made me sound like a monster who wanted to beat up women for fun and she kept going on and on. Then she said in disgust, 'Does it hurt when you get punched?'

And I said, 'Of course it fucking hurts, I'm a boxer.' Swearing on live breakfast TV wasn't a good thing for me to do but she was just relentless, like she wanted me to crack, and in the end I did. I let myself down, I know I did. When she started insulting me and telling me I was a disgrace to women I just snapped.

'I can fight and I am fighting but that doesn't mean every woman has to if they don't want to. No one is making anyone box.' Of course, it was TV gold. Paula Yates was laughing her head off in the background and everyone around was either in stunned silence or calling out frantically, 'Cut, cut!'

What should have been such positive and momentous publicity was nothing more than a witch-hunt really. Everything felt like a personal attack and I was just being used for ratings, for audience figures, as talking points. I didn't know it at the time of course, I just went from one interview to the next. They didn't give a fuck about me. Vanessa didn't care that she was so hurtful when she called me disgusting and vile and not ladylike. I am a real person yet no one seemed to remember that. I had feelings and I had pride and all I had dreamt of doing was boxing in this country. But people didn't realise they were ruining my dream. I didn't understand why people couldn't see that.

Anything bad that was written about me didn't just affect me either, Mum was reading stuff about her daughter that was hurtful to the whole family. But she never let it show how much it upset her.

'You know what love, it will be tomorrow's chip paper,' she said, full of bravado. She didn't want me to give in. She never wanted me to succumb to bullies.

'Whatever you've got to do, just keep doing it,' she said. 'Don't worry about what they write, you're only boxing, you're not killing anyone!' Which for Mum to say was quite profound as she hated me boxing. She didn't want her daughter getting battered and she didn't watch any fights. She'd pretend she would but she didn't want to know. But she still supported my right to do it and she never once asked me to quit. And Dad was the same, he told me to just ignore all the press and he'd remind me of everyone in Fleetwood, all our friends and family and people who supported me 100 per cent. Even if it felt like the world was against me, I had support at home.

And it only got worse when I officially applied for my boxing licence again. The freak show labels came out in force and there were calls for me to go to America to box, no one wanted me here I was told. I can't remember who wrote that but I can tell you of two people that were more outspoken than most, more savage and more ferocious than anyone else.

'I think it's absolutely disgusting that women are being allowed to fight. If anything happens during a women's fight there will be calls for a ban and all those left-wing, do-gooder lesbians who have been fighting Jane Couch's case will be the first to complain. The only women you'll find in a ring at one of my fights are very pretty ring-card girls.' So said Frank Maloney, boxing promoter and then manager of WBC world heavyweight champion Lennox Lewis. Frank Maloney is now Kellie Maloney after gender reassignment surgery. Frank is now female. I'll leave that irony with you.

The Frank Maloney I knew back then was the most brutal, vicious and anti-women boxing promoter I was ever going to meet. He was a huge name in the boxing world and one of the biggest promoters in the UK.

The number of radio interviews I did with him in the studio as well was unreal. It seemed that no one wanted to hear the positive and exciting new era of women's boxing, they just wanted an argument. The radio producers knew what made listeners tune in and if I was on the show the chances were Frank would be too, making sure everyone knew why women's boxing was horrific and why I was a freak for wanting to do it.

Tex would set me up too. It was all publicity to him. He would say to me, 'Jane, you have a phone call,' casual as anything, and it would be a three-way conversation with a presenter from Radio 5 and Maloney on the phone and I would be in this argument that I didn't want to be in.

Or I would be heading into a radio station for what I thought was a one-to-one interview and Frank would just be sitting there, already being all pally and jokey with the radio host, like they both knew I was only here to provide the entertainment. And if I would ask, 'What is he doing here?' they would always come back with, 'We're just having a debate about whether women should box.'

'That's fine,' I'd say, 'but why is he here?'

'He's the objective side,' they said, stopping short of saying he's the voice of reason. It was either Frank Maloney or Frank Warren, another boxing promoter, I would be arguing with. Maloney more-so; it was like he wanted to be the one up against me except we weren't in a boxing ring, this was a public showdown and he already had the public on his side because they hated me and what I stood for. I lost the fight before I had even begun each time.

It seemed to happen every time I went into a TV or radio station, one of the Franks was there. And I would always end up having a stand-up row with them because they were clever and they'd provoke me and push my buttons and I'd be trying to tell the world about what vile characters they were, all the time knowing it was doing no good, no one was on my side. I'd think to myself, all these programmes, they are just an argument, they don't give a fuck that I'm trying to make a living, they just want an argument, to get listeners or to get headlines. Maloney would say I was a freak, it was medically wrong, it was disgusting and totally disrespecting women and they'd have people ringing up and agreeing with him.

It was exhausting and it was getting me nowhere. I stopped doing such argumentative shows after a while. It was the same thing over and over again and I began to finally realise I was just being used to get in more listeners or get more audience figures. But they were so clever, the journalists and the TV or radio producers, about having me on their show. And whatever I said did no good, I'd get so pissed off that I think several times I'd just let them rant at me, not bothering to rise to the bait. 'What's the point of me being on the end of this phone?' I'd say. 'You don't give a fuck what I say, you're not interested.' Or I'd go one step further, one step too far, and say, 'Just shut your fucking mouth Frank!' and that would be gold to them. Of course I was a thug, labelled a bully, a freak again, no normal person would speak like that, would they?

In the end, I felt like I was constantly fighting a losing battle. I couldn't defend women's boxing, I couldn't defend myself. No one wanted to hear it. I can't make you like something you don't like, I can't make you like women's boxing any more than I can make you like anything else. The point was, why couldn't I just be allowed to get on and do it? What did it matter to anyone else? I felt like I had been thrown to the wolves and no one wanted to save me. Every time I'd tell someone like Maloney or Warren, or Vanessa or whoever to 'fuck off' because I heard the same thing over and over again it was another point to them. It made me look like an idiot, it made me look bad and wrong and it was just amusing to them.

I have nearly come to proper blows with Maloney on several occasions. We were both in a TV studio once and the hatred he had for me seemed to just radiate off him like a force. He came right up to my face, was toe-to-toe with me, and was just so angry. 'Fuck off Frank,' I said, 'or if you want to hit me, hit me, go on ...' I knew I was goading him but I didn't care. But he couldn't physically hit me so he carried on hitting me with his vile and abusive rhetoric instead. He's spat at me before, called me pretty much every name under the sun, and I have probably never felt so much hatred towards one person in my whole life.

But now? Now I'd quite happily have a coffee with him. He means absolutely nothing to me. I have no feelings towards him whatsoever now.

All this media interest after the court case kept up as the press followed me getting my actual licence. I had to apply for it in the same way as Sara asked me to all those months ago.

But this time, of course, the board weren't able to do anything to stop it going through. I went through exactly the same process as before and travelled once again to the interview meeting where I was surrounded by all the ex-managers, trainers and boxers. There was an extra air of animosity in the room, of abhorrence. None of them wanted to give me a licence but none of them could stop me getting one. I sat there, answering all their questions politely, 'Yes, no, yes, no, OK ...' before they finally said, 'We'll grant you the licence.' But it was through gritted teeth. And they couldn't help but slot in a jibe or two.

'We don't know what you're trying to achieve,' they said.. 'It won't last, you won't get anywhere, no one will promote you. You'll be on your own.'

And they weren't wrong.

It seemed as if the board were in control and had sent out the same message to every promoter (and they were all men) in England: she'll never box here. I felt completely frozen out and I had nowhere to go.

I just wanted to concentrate on fighting but I was doing interview after interview after interview and trying to justify why women should be allowed to box, and yet here I was unable to actually box anywhere anyway. I got sick of it. I wished I was back with Sara and Dinah and taking on the world again because they were the most unbelievable women I had ever met. If it wasn't for them there wouldn't be any women boxing, I completely believe that. They took on the giants and made them crumble and we felt like such an unstoppable team together, completely invincible. And now I was on my own and I felt vulnerable. I was exhausted by constantly trying to justify what I did, and now this licence, which technically gave me the ability to fight in the UK, felt like a poisoned chalice. All the promoters shut down on me because of their close association with the board. 'Women's boxing will get bigger in this country and we don't want that do we?' seemed to be the common theme between them. Like they were hoping if they made it hard enough for me to fight here, I'd just fuck off to America or Germany. The only one person I had who agreed to promote one of my fights was a man called Joey Pyle Jr. He did what he wanted and he was the only promoter to take me on because he couldn't care less what the board wanted him to do.

The press, having seized on the fact that I had now officially been granted a licence and a women's boxing fight would be imminent, began to speculate about the brutality of such a spectacle on their doorstep. The BBBC were rubbing their hands with glee as they knew full well they had the press on their side, and that was their power.

This Morning did a poll with the question, 'Should I be allowed to compete or not?' There was a phone-in with viewers ringing in giving their tuppence-worth on my sporting career, and the overwhelming consensus was no, no I shouldn't be allowed to compete. I can't remember the exact percentage but it was pretty conclusive to the then hosts, Richard and Judy, as they revealed the public vote. No one wanted me to box. The media didn't like it, the public didn't like it. It was like this big hate campaign. I remember being in Asda one day and an elderly woman came over to me and got all cross and indignant with me. 'I don't know why you want to box,' she seethed, 'you're making women look bad you are!'

Steve Presnail, the boxing promoter who I had known since being at the farm, tried to get me some sponsorship deals, earn me some extra money while I wasn't boxing, but that was a joke in itself. No one wanted to go near me. I was still not an athlete, or a pioneer, or a champion. I was a freak.

It felt like I was in the Dark Ages, not on the eve of the new millennium, and the problem was, the more I read and heard I was a monster and shameful to other women and a thug ... the more I believed it.

Chapter Eight

Fighting on British soil

'The quest for credibility remains female boxing's toughest fight of all.'

The Independent, November 1998

BY the ime I went back to the farm I think I stayed in for about 11 months. I just couldn't cope. My face was in the papers on a regular basis as this new monster, so I just kept my head down, kept on training and tried not to draw attention to myself. I didn't have the energy to do anything else, all the press backlash had eaten away at me and I felt completely deflated. From winning the court case I was now in serious training to fight my first boxing match on English soil.

The BBC posted an online article that at least seemed to agree with what I had been saying all this time. I was fighting a new battle just to get a fight: 'Couch's problem is getting the big UK promoters – Frank Warren, Frank Maloney, Barry Hearn – to put her on their shows. So far, all have baulked. Maloney told BBC News Online: "Women should stay in the kitchen, or in the bedroom. I bet he would not say that to Jane Couch."' Ha! If only they knew! Of course he'd say it to me, he's said a lot worse. But it was a hint that perhaps I had a bit of support.

My first UK fight was to be fought in November, only a few months after winning the court case, and was scheduled to take part at Caesar's, a well-known nightclub in Streatham, south London. Roy Cameron, another boxing promoter who, like Joey, didn't bow to the board, was responsible for setting up the night. My opponent was Simona Lukic, an 18-year-old from Germany who had won a few matches but not many. I knew she was OK but I knew I had to prove that I was better.

One of Frank Maloney's boxers was on the same bill as me and when he found out that was the case he was furious. He pulled his boxer off the show.

I wonder if he had hoped that the board were going to ask me to come off the bill, but they didn't so he just removed his boxer instead. That's how much he hated me boxing.

'In my opinion all officials should have boycotted it and I take my hat off to those officials at the Boxing Board of Control who have declined to work the show.'

I was seething. And not just for me, for the boxer he had brought to take part in a fight who now wasn't going to get paid because his promoter didn't want him fighting the same night as a woman. I couldn't believe he was taking food out of that kid's mouth, denying him the right to earn money, to provide for his family, all because of me? I had heard some shit in my time from Frank but now it was affecting the lives of other boxers it reached a whole new level.

It wasn't an isolated incident, of course, the fights I had after this one around the UK were similar experiences. I remember one of the male boxers coming up to me at a venue devastated as he'd been pulled from the bill that night. He needed the money, he said, he couldn't afford not to fight. So I asked him why he wasn't and he said it was because of me! Because I was fighting!

The night of my fight in Caesar's got a lot of attention, and quite rightly so. The place was absolutely heaving, I could hear the noise of the crowd from the dressing room as Tex taped up my hands. You couldn't get a ticket for love nor money apparently, there were over 1,500 packed into the club and I was so pleased. This felt like support, proper support for me, at last. People were here to watch women boxing, I had made that happen. I had to forget all the bad press, all the negative, I had won the right to be here, I was going to bloody enjoy being the home boxer for a change!

When I walked out to the ring the place was just buzzing, absolutely buzzing. There were so many camera crews and photographers there and the audience was filled with people from all walks of life – young, old and loads and loads of women too. It was brilliant to see, it took away a lot of the hurt of the previous few months. Even if they never pick up a boxing glove in their lives, I've made it possible for them to do it if they want to, that's what I have to remember.

The fight itself was over in just under three minutes. The referee stopped the fight halfway through the second round as I had completely blasted Lukic. She wasn't fighting back to my barrage, and in the end the ref, Richie Davies, stopped the fight. 'I treated them exactly the same as I would male fighters,' he said. 'My main priority is their welfare, that's why I stopped it.'

Ironically, John Morris, the secretary of the BBBC, was the first to congratulate me afterwards. Another big moment I thought, and then read what he said in the papers the next day: 'It's an historic night for British boxing but I haven't the foggiest about where women's boxing goes from here.' Back to square one it seemed.

'The German girl's too pretty to be a boxer. She looks more like an aerobics instructor,' said someone ringside to a reporter.

'Women's boxing didn't need this, a damaging blow to an already fragile credibility,' came some of the press reports after my fight. And 'It's not about boxing, people have come here for a circus,' said Kevin Lueshing, a former British welterweight champion.

There was criticism towards Roy Cameron, over his choice of my opponent. But most of the backlash was again directed at me.

OK, Lukic wasn't great, but she had beaten other people. When other girls who fought after me boxed tomato cans (easy opponents), that was OK, the reporting was all about what brilliant fighters they were. But when I fought Lukic, who wasn't particularly hard to beat, it was 'a disgusting spectacle that didn't last two rounds.' We had sold the place out for crying out loud and yet there was still no let-up from the media and the boxing circle. I remember celebrating my socks off after that fight, enjoying a bit of a release, and we all went out in London afterwards.

Mum and Dad had come to see the fight, although I know Mum didn't actually watch, she wouldn't. Dad on the other hand was dressed up with his Union Jack flag around his shoulders, telling everyone I was his daughter, shouting and cheering around the ring like a mad lunatic! I think he was trying to impress all the women who'd come to watch with the line, 'I'm Jane's dad! I'm Jane's dad!'

Mum was always pleased when the fighting was over and joined in the celebrations afterwards, although she tried to keep things civilised.

'Come on then,' she'd say after the fight, as a big group of us went out to celebrate, 'we'll just get some food and get an early night.'

And I was buzzing, the adrenaline still pumping through my veins and I wanted to go out all night and she'd be like, 'No, come on love, let's go and get an early night'. That protectiveness. That is what she felt. I am sure my mum always thought I would grow out of this, out of wanting to fight. When we went back to Fleetwood after that fight I was bombarded, completely bombarded. It was like I was a returning hero and the fans and support I got there was incredible. They cared about me, I was their champion and that felt bloody great. Everywhere I went back home I was stopped and people wanted to chat or ask me questions or have a photo. I think it probably drove Mum mad, all this attention from the fans and media, but in my mind it was all part of the job, something I just dealt with, and I must admit it was nice to deal with more positive local news stories and press! And when Tex told me that the editor of *Boxing News* described my debut as having 'exceeded interest shown in either Lennox Lewis or Naseem Hamed, when they made their professional debuts in this country,' that was all I needed to hear.

I think I boxed Wembley after my first licensed fight, then Middlesbrough, Aston Villa and Elephant & Castle. Fighting on familiar territory was great at first, I was finally able to earn a living in England and I was able to add two more titles to my name as well, the WIBF welterweight title at the beginning of 1999 and the WBF lightweight title at the end of that same year.

And then, almost as soon as it happened, it was all over again. The fights and the promotions in this country just dried up. It became a battle again to get fights, it seemed that everyone (including me) had been swept up in me boxing in this country and now the furore had died down, everything went back to the way it was. It was like the promoters thought, 'Fuck it, we've done our bit, we don't need to put her on anymore.' And for a fighter to get fights, they need to sell tickets. I had to be able to sell over 500 tickets to cover the opponent's wage, and OK I had a goodish following in Fleetwood and family and friends but it was hard selling that number of tickets to people who, once they had seen a female fight, were almost of the opinion they had 'ticked' a life-experience box. The drama was over, no one needed the headlines anymore. And my heart just felt broken all over again.

All your energy and enthusiasm goes out of it then and I started to think why do I bother? Why am I constantly battling to get fights, to sell tickets to prove ... well, to prove what? I was still getting told I couldn't fight in England, even if it wasn't directly. I had a licence, that was still mine, so they couldn't stop me that way, I was just being told through other means

But I wasn't going to stop boxing, I was determined, probably even more so, that I would carry on fighting abroad and I would fight in the big bouts in the big casinos and carry on just as before. 'Fuck the lot of you,' I thought, childishly but honestly. I flew back to Connecticut and Foxwoods Casino to fight American boxer Liz Mueller.

The morning of that fight I saw Barry Hearn, then promoter with Prince Naseem Hamed, who was topping the bill. Being on the undercard to Naz meant that it was going to be another huge occasion – not only was this fight on the American TV networks but it was going to be shown on Sky too. And although I had accepted this fight at short notice – this was becoming a common occurrence – having just come from several wins back in England, I felt confident. I had a good chat with Barry at breakfast the morning of the fight. He was pretty impressed that I had taken it at such short notice and we started talking about money and how much I was getting paid. And after I told him, he just got out his wallet and gave me $500. I first of all thought, 'Bloody hell, that's nice!' before I started wondering how much should I have been getting if he felt sorry enough for me to give me that? How much were the male boxers getting paid?

While my boxing wasn't making headlines, I was still in and out of the papers when they needed a villain to a story.

It's important you don't misunderstand me completely here, I am not saying I'm a saint or never said anything bad or provoking or deliberately goading on occasion. I am well aware I have a potty mouth and sometimes when I say to people in a jokey way, 'Oh fuck off will ya!' that it can sound rude and offensive. But people who know me, the folks that have known me for years, will know that's just me! I'll say 'fuck off' to anyone in a jokey manner, that's just what I do, who I am. It's my natural reaction if you like and I will quite often swear and take the piss out of people because it's never serious. 'Oh, you're not coming to see my fight? Go on with you then, fuck off!'

I didn't help myself, I know that, quite often if Tex was asking me to comment on something I'd just tell him to write what he wanted. I had absolutely no interest in the media side of anything.

And every time it went quiet for me, he'd make sure the media remembered my name.

'Jane Couch in legal battle for right to fight a man,' screamed one headline.

'Couch is willing to fight a man,' reported another. This was the latest story and it had come about because of a new BBBC regulation that made it really hard for foreign fighters to box over here. Basically, in June 2001, I fought at Wembley against a Croatian opponent. It wasn't for a title, just an exhibition match that was supposed to have happened the previous year but the BBBC threw a spanner in the works. It was now their ruling that foreign boxers had to have their medical tests completed in the

UK before they could fight over here. So any medicals and tests and scans they had already completed in their own country that made them eligible to fight, didn't count in this country as the BBBC wanted to complete their own medical examinations. It was a huge problem for small promoters trying to bring in women fighters from other countries and it seemed like the board were making it harder and harder to get women over for fighting. When there are only a few British-born fighters ready to fight, there isn't much competition!

It was so frustrating. It looked like all the tickets I had already secured as sold at Wembley would go to waste as I couldn't find an opponent who was willing to pay out for all the medical tests here. Don't get me wrong, a physical exam is a necessity in boxing, of course it is, but why all of a sudden a boxer's own medical team from their own country are deemed untrustworthy doesn't make any sense to me. No one would put their own boxer in danger.

So the story went out that unless a suitable opponent could be found in time for my Wembley fight, I would make 'British boxing history by fighting a man'. Tex released a statement to the media that he knew mixed the right amount of headline-grabbing quotes to get people talking again. And it did. 'There's nothing in the board's rules saying that a woman cannot fight a man, although now we've tested the water they'll probably come up with one,' he said. 'We want to take the board to court next week and either force them to sanction this fight or give their reasons for refusing to allow it. Jane is a fighter being denied the opportunity of pursuing her trade. When she received her licence it was never on the understanding that she couldn't fight a man.'

It was typical Tex, he talked the talk but it would be me getting the battering – from the media and the public again – in the end. Of course I don't have a problem fighting men, I was sparring with them day in and day out at training, it didn't faze me one bit. Tex knew if asked my thoughts on fighting a man I'd respond with that sort of cockiness. It was a win-win situation for him. I never said I wanted to fight a man in a public boxing match and I had no idea about taking the BBBC to court again but boxing a man was the norm for me and if any journalist asked or questioned me, that was the response I would give. I had no problem with it and he knew I'd go along with it. I tended to go along with all these things, it was just easier to agree.

'I don't want to let people down, it would mean a hell of a lot to me to appear at Wembley,' I said. 'I've sold a hell of a lot of tickets and don't want to let people down. I'd go into that ring with exactly the same attitude I have when fighting a woman, although it would be particularly satisfying to beat a bloke. I went through a long drawn-out process to get my licence and now the gloves are off for another court case.'

The board put out a reply and they knew, even though we were never going to take them to court, they would win.

'Jane asked if she could box an exhibition against a man,' said Simon Block, the board's general secretary. 'But that is not something we would permit. Neither would we approve of a woman sparring men in public.'

It all died down in the end when my fight against my Croatian opponent, Viktoria Oliynyk, did take place at Wembley and I won. I would fight and beat her again a few years later, fairly convincingly.

The following month, in July 2001, I flew out to Montego Bay in Jamaica. I should never have agreed to such a last-minute fight, but I did and I found myself on a long-haul flight from England knowing that I would have just seven hours before my fight. That was bloody tough I can tell you. I was fighting American boxer Tim Witherspoon's sister-in-law, Carla 'Shakurah' Witherspoon. Tim was a regular sparring partner for Muhammad Ali and two-time world heavyweight champion, so I knew if she had spent any time under his watchful eye I'd be in for a tough fight. He also trained his son, Tim Witherspoon Jr, so he was obviously keen to make a successful transition from world-class boxer to trainer and keep up the positive reputation, and I'm sure he would have tried to help Carla any way he could.

I did try to find out what I could about her and discovered she had boxed some solid opposition, like Leah Mellinger, before so as well as being jet-lagged, I didn't feel particularly prepared for it. Tex was just saying yes to everything, however short notice it was. It wasn't the first time this had happened and I was finding it increasingly hard to summon up the energy and mental strength to jump from match to match. And now here I was in the Caribbean having only been fighting a few weeks previously, just got off a long flight and now expected to box in a boiling-hot country.

As soon as we came out from the airport the intense heat just hit me, it's like a full-on, knockout encounter as soon as you step outside. I needed to cool down, get some kip in the hotel and then I'd find the venue for the match.

We jumped in a waiting taxi and the driver was chatting the whole time, and then when he realised that I was a boxer and had come over here for a fight, he made sure he made a bit of a detour.

'Look Jane, that's where you're boxing tomorrow,' he said.

And I couldn't work out what he was pointing out. I could only see a beautiful sandy beach.

'Where?' I said.

'There!' and he pointed again in the direction of the sand.

'That's the beach,' I said, wondering if I was completely jet-lagged and missing the point altogether.

'Yeah, yeah, that's where you're boxing,' he was grinning at me, 'there on the beach!'

'It's a hundred and twenty fucking degrees outside!' I said, turning to Tex. 'What the fuck?!'

'Oh you'll be alright,' was the response. It had come to be a fairly standard response from Tex whatever my situation.

You're coming off a long-haul flight and in less than seven hours you'll be boxing outside in extreme heat? You'll be alright.

You're fighting two matches back to back? You'll be alright.

Your best mate from childhood has been killed at sea but you need to carry on with your fight. You'll be alright.

The press, half the country and the majority of promoters want to see you fail and are willing you to be KOd at Wembley. You'll be alright.

I hadn't done any heat training or preparation at all and I was staggered that I was being put in this situation. It was so hot it was a miracle that we didn't suffer from any sort of heat stroke or worse. I even had to have a blood test before the fight as the medical that I undertook before we flew out wasn't accepted so they wanted to test me again. My dressing room was a little makeshift shack on the beach and the electricity ran out as Tex was trying to strap my hands.

We had help though, Lennox Lewis was in the country visiting his mum who lived a few streets behind the beach where we were fighting. He had called Tex earlier so he knew we were here and he called in to see us. He had impeccable timing as he arrived just as the lights in our hut went out and he ended up holding a couple of candles for Tex so he could carry on wrapping my hands.

That was a tough fight, not just with the intense heat but Witherspoon was a strong opponent. In the end, it went four rounds and the judges' decision was unanimous, I was the winner. I would normally celebrate a win like that and see more of the place I was boxing in, but I was exhausted and I couldn't wait to get paid, get back to the airport and head home for a rest and a cool down. But we didn't get paid; the promoter came in to see us after the fight and explained that the prize money had been dropped and he didn't have money to pay us. As he was saying it, in such a raw display of intimidation, he stuck this massive knife into the wooden table in front of us.

'Fine, fine mate, you're alright, don't worry about it!' I stammered, I couldn't get the words out quick enough at the sight of the knife. It was the scariest thing I had ever encountered, we were on our own on the beach and being confronted by a man and his knife. We weren't going to make any trouble, I just wanted to leave. But I was furious when we got to the airport. Tex wasn't to know that the promoter would threaten us with a sodding knife but it just seemed, yet again, I was just being asked to push myself to the limit physically and mentally and for absolutely no benefit. I would never fight half-heartedly, I can't do that, that isn't me, that isn't why I wanted to box. I will never give anything but my all for each fight and Tex knew that, but still I was being asked to keep my side of the bargain and get nothing back.

Tex wasn't angry on my behalf, furious that his boxer was being treated so unfairly. It was just as if he expected it in a way. He was always saying to me to just carry on doing what I was doing and not to worry about not getting paid, there is always a next time.

I have known a lot of managers over the years and Tex wasn't an exception to the rule. You get the odd ex-fighter who has retired from boxing and become a manager and they are the good ones because they don't want their boxers to go through what they had to go through.

But nine times out of ten, the managers are just in it for themselves. Boxers have a really short shelf life so we mean nothing in the grand scheme of things. The mangers and promoters, they are the ones who are around forever. You could have a manager who looks after hundreds of boxers in his career but he might only get success with one or two. What happens to the rest? Thanks very much, see you, bye now! There are ex-boxers homeless on the streets because they have retired and then been hung out to dry. What happens next? There is no support, no aftercare ... they are just left. And a lot of them have nothing else, have known nothing else other than boxing and are used to being told they are the most important thing in their manager's eyes, but then ... then they are cast aside and forgotten. They're no use to the managers or promoters anymore and it's so hard for them to find their way in life. To have a purpose, to make sense of the world again after being in that bubble. The bubble bursts. A lot of ex-boxers, if you saw them now ... it's just heart-breaking.

They sold their souls to the managers who used them and worked them hard and pushed them to train and then cast them aside. So what do you do? You're not qualified for anything, what are your options? You've spent so many hours, days, weeks training and putting your heart and soul into this world that just disregards you so easily in the end. Then you leave the bubble and step out again into the sun and think, is that it? You don't have anyone telling you what to eat, when to sleep, when to train, what you should weigh, who to box and all of a sudden ... what?

This isn't just an odd few cases either, it seems to be the way the boxing world operates and has operated for years. And I can't make sense of it any more than you can, but I think it's worth bringing it to your attention because the more people are aware of what is happening, the more people can help – the more people can reach out and offer support, the more people can stand up and say, 'Hang on, that's not right ... let's do something about this.'

Training at the farm was non-stop. This was my job, I had to give it my all every second of the day. Two months before I had a big fight I would be working on my stamina, doing bag work, skipping, light circuit training and sparring. As I am a lightweight fighter I need to keep my body weight down so I wouldn't do much weightlifting. As a fight got closer, my training became more and more intense and my days were pretty much the same – skipping, shadow-boxing, sit-ups, press-ups, more sparring, more skipping, more bag work – until just a few weeks before and I eased off slightly to prevent injury. I cut sparring ten days before a fight in case I cut my hands, and in the last couple of days I tried to do nothing but focus on the job in hand, focus on my fight, so I was physically and mentally strong and ready.

That is how it is meant to happen. That is how I should prepare. Yet it wasn't always the case. Two years after my Caribbean fight I was facing one of the best female fighters who has ever walked the earth. Even today, no one will ever match Lucia Rijker, she is a phenomenal fighter and Tex told me I was due to compete with her just 12 days before our fight – 12 days' notice against one of the best boxers in the world. The bout was in Los Angeles at the Staples Center and I was stupid to accept it, but I was full of bravado too. And I didn't embarrass myself, I took her to the full eight rounds and ended up losing on points. I was so cross, I had lost on points but only had under two weeks to prepare. If I had had three months' notice I would have beaten her! Taking the fight was my decision and mine alone but I shouldn't have done it. Or Tex should have talked me out of it but I did it as I had to put food in my mouth.

Rijker was a massive star and I knew even if I didn't beat her I would push her close. Plus it was a dream to fight someone like her as she will go down as the greatest woman fighter ever, even now, even with all the women fighters, they wouldn't lace her boots she was so brilliant.

I don't remember a lot about that fight other than being in a lot of pain in the seventh round. She landed two powerful hits to the side of my head just before the bell sounded and this noise in my ear was unbelievable. My eardrum was perforated and I stumbled back to the corner in a complete daze. All I could hear was this deafening whooshing noise and I thought I had brain damage, I have never experienced such pain in my life, and I didn't feel I had any control over my body and my legs to move me back to Tex. I couldn't hear anything else other than the air sound that was thundering out of my ears. I felt and looked like a complete drunk as I was stumbling all over the place. I had no balance whatsoever.

And in that moment I had no idea what was happening to me, all I could hear was that air sound, and as I was walking I was stumbling as I looked drunk because I had no balance. That noise in my head was just thunderous as I went back to the corner, and I was trying to sit down and I couldn't even do that. I was falling over as I got to the stool and I just shouted to Tex, 'I can't, I can't hear.' I was trying to keep my head up but I just wanted to wrap my hands around my ears, which of course I couldn't because of my clothes. And I sat down, put my head down and Tex was right in front of me, telling me, 'You'll be alright, you'll be alright.' So I carried on. But losing your balance in boxing, once that goes, that's it. So it went to the final round and I lost.

* * *

My world title fight against Jaime Clampitt in 2004 was memorable for two reasons. I won the NABA and IWBF junior welterweight titles from the Canadian champion and I got to hang out in New York afterwards!

The bout was at Foxwoods Casino again and being back in America was testament to how much they seemed to enjoy my fights. They were good to watch, there was no denying that, and Americans loved the entertainment. Ricky Hatton was in America at the time, taking part in his own big match in Las Vegas, and we spoke to each other a few days before. I called his agent, Paul, to wish him luck and he held the phone up so I could hear Ricky shout back to me, 'Good luck to you an' all!'

I had become mates with Ricky and Paul over the years and neither of them liked women boxing. Ricky couldn't watch me do it but he always respected me for doing it and having the right to do it. I don't like ice skating but I'd never tell someone that they couldn't do it. Having Ricky's respect meant a lot to me. It meant a lot to get a good luck before a world championship title fight and it still means a lot to know I have him in my corner. To have people like him when you feel like you are fighting a losing battle, to get his support when it feels like the world is against you, that means a lot.

And they would never, ever say to me not to do it. They wouldn't ever disagree with a woman's right to box. They just didn't like it. And that's OK, they respected me as an athlete and a boxer. I couldn't change their opinion any more than I could change their opinion on what type of beer they liked or their favourite cereal. You can't change anyone's opinion, however much you try. I learnt that the hard way.

Our fight was scrappy but strong and went to ten rounds, with the crowd on their feet several times that night. It was a well-matched, great women's fight that I won fairly convincingly. Interestingly, I was starting to get press attention for other reasons than me being a woman. I was now an old woman! I was 35 years old and they were saying I wasn't going to win the title. But I did, and I was going to bring back the belt to prove it.

That's not to say our fight wasn't brutal, she punched me in the mouth in the early rounds and cracked my first tooth. It was hanging on by a thread and was all chipped and after the fight I was in a lot of pain. After the match I was getting myself sorted in the changing rooms when Jaime's manager, Jimmy Burchfield came in.

'Hey man, you comin' out for a drink?'

I was in so much pain with my tooth, I couldn't face it.

But he had a solution to that and told me to go up to the seventh floor, room 1719 and knock on the door. 'My dentist is there,' he said, then left the dressing room. And I was thinking, who has a dentist on call at 11pm at night? But I went up there and knocked on the door.

'Jimmy sent me,' I said, when the door opened.

'What's wrong with you?'

'My tooth is cracked and I'm in such fucking pain … I can hardly talk I'm in that much pain,' I said.

And then he got out this little pipe and said to me, 'Here, have that.'

And I breathed it in.

'Pain gone?'

'Yeah it's gone,' I said.

'Right,' he said, 'go and see your dentist when you go back to England.'

And that was that! I was fucking high as a kite for the rest of the night! I was completely out of it but in no pain so went out in New York with Jimmy and some others he was out with, some of the big promoters from South Africa. God knows what the dentist had given me but I literally had no pain, I was just completely numb!

My tooth was still wobbly as it was hanging on by the nerves but I didn't care and had a thoroughly wicked night out.

Jaime lost her sponsorship deal after that, but they didn't give it to me, they only brought me over to America for a good fight, I still didn't deserve anything else. That was just the way of the business, no one really cared, I was getting a raw deal once again. At the time, I think I was living off my own ego, my own hype, and it's only now I am out of this bubble I can see I have just been chewed up and spat out.

I had just boxed in this massive televised fight in America, in one of the world's biggest casinos, given it my heart and soul and come away with a world title and I came back to England thinking there would be some sort of celebration, some sort of congratulations, but there was nothing. I think people thought I'd been sitting in the pub for the past 12 weeks or so. No one knew what was happening as I wasn't fighting in this country and the matches weren't shown on telly over here, so when it went quiet they probably all thought, 'Oh, she's having a break.' And that couldn't be further from the truth! No, I am working my arse off in training to fight a good fight in a country that will put me on a bill and I got to the point where I just thought why am I fucking bothering. I was fed up of leaving the country to fight but coming home from America with a world title that didn't make anyone proud. No one gave a shit.

It's different nowadays and it's bloody brilliant. Even crap, half-hearted matches that I've watched on the TV now, everyone is reporting in a positive and encouraging way. 'Didn't she do well?' that sort of thing, even though to my mind it was a crap fight, she got hammered, she put up no resistance ... but, then again, the fact that they are being positive, that's fine. That's how it should be. It just wasn't that way with me.

Chapter Nine

Royal encounters

'You're not as bashed up as I was expecting!'

HRH Prince of Wales

IN 2007 I was back in Connecticut and back in the ring against Jaime Clampitt. Having won another world title and defended a previous one the last time I fought her, I knew she'd be chomping at the bit to get even. I had satisfied the press and the crowd the last time we boxed with a win when they had all been calling me too old and over the hill. And now it was time for Jaime to have her rematch and she made sure that I knew, right from the first bell, that she meant business. I lost the fight. It went to the full ten rounds and in the end the judges found in her favour. She came out strong but I didn't back down, I thought I was stronger in a few of the rounds at the end, but in the end the decision went to her. At least I didn't need more dental work after this fight.

Having been on the receiving end of some of the worst and most degrading press attention I was ever likely to get, 2007 saw a bit of a tide turn when the Queen's birthday honours list was revealed and my name was among those receiving an MBE, Member of the Order of the British Empire. It's given for 'Outstanding achievement or service to the community that will have had a long-term, significant impact and will stand out as an example to others.' It was like getting a right hook from Mike Tyson, I was absolutely knocked off my feet when the letter came through to the farm. But when you get the letter, it doesn't say you've got the MBE for certain, only that you've been nominated for one. Then the honours list is made official and the media, which had hounded me, degraded me, humiliated me, shamed me and slated me at every turn, descended on the farm with congratulations.

I was in complete shock. Not only was I getting an MBE for Services to Boxing, I was being complimented, greeted with praise by the piranhas from the press who now all wanted a piece of me because I was being recognised as someone who was making a difference. It was nearly ten years since I had been hounded for wanting to get a licence to box in this country and now Her Majesty wanted to bestow an honour on me for actually making it happen. For nearly a decade I had been going up against everyone in order to fight and now the tide had turned and it seemed I had blazed a trail and opened minds to women's boxing and was being congratulated for it.

So I think a part of me was like, really? It's so ironic isn't it? 'Services to Boxing' and yet no one would give me a fucking chance, not even a little tiny bit of credit in the beginning, when no one understood my ambition, when I was jeered at for having a passion that wasn't deemed 'normal'.

But I was over the moon. Me, Jane Couch, Fleetwood Assassin, going to Buckingham Palace and getting an MBE?! I should have put a bet on that when Dave Smith first taught me how to gamble all those years ago!

And the press, well, they were now better, kind. 'Fair play for getting that' was the general consensus from them. And if anything, I used their new-found allegiance to my advantage. Getting an MBE and having the press on my side was a two fingers up to Frank Maloney I suppose. Let him put that in his anti-women boxing pipe and smoke it.

The day I received my MBE from Prince Charles was just so surreal. I think I had to keep pinching myself as I still couldn't believe I was actually in Buckingham Palace – Buckingham Palace! Mum had come with me, she had travelled down from Fleetwood and met me in Bristol before we both travelled to London.

She loves the royal family, so she was buzzing with excitement. Although she didn't make a big deal of it at first, it was like I had told her I had earned a Girl Guide badge or something, not an MBE. 'Well, you've worked hard for it,' she said, and that was it! But I knew she was over the moon. I'm pretty sure she told everyone she knew in Fleetwood that her Jane was going to go to Buckingham Palace to meet Prince Charles!

In many ways, the day was probably more special for her as she had seen me go through everything to get to this moment. I had lived it of course, but watching someone you love go through the hell of wanting to fight, actually fighting and then being told they were the lowest form of female savage because they wanted to fight ... well, I knew Mum took a lot of what was said to heart. And I knew she never wanted me to fight, she could never and will never to this day understand it but she was always behind me, backing me, supporting me, every step of the way, from the moment she talked to Tom and me about leaving Fleetwood and making a life away from the fishing community – a life away from what was expected of us. We could have so easily fallen into that world simply because that is what we grew up surrounded by. But she never expected it or wanted it for us so we dreamt bigger and we did bigger things. And as we walked up the steps into the palace I was so damn proud of her for encouraging us to have dreams and never give up on them. Even though I'm sure if you asked her, having a daughter who was a boxer wasn't quite what she meant!

It was so humbling being in the palace, there is an air of prestige, of grandeur, of unrivalled uniqueness ... it's very difficult to explain, even now, what that moment felt like. The surroundings are just so breathtakingly beautiful; Mum wanted to spend hours looking around and taking everything in, but things run like clockwork in the palace and I had to go to the Gallery Room upstairs and be taken through the running order and the rules of the day. And there are a lot of rules to remember!

We had to line up in a queue and at that moment I felt on edge and immediately surrounded by well-to-do people who seemed to be far more at home in these surroundings than a boxer from Fleetwood. There was a woman in front of me, I don't know who she was but she was very posh and she was talking to the lady in front of her. I heard her say, 'I got my dress from Harrods', and I just thought, 'Oh fucking hell, please don't talk to me.' I hated that sort of snobbery and I had no time for it. But it's like if you're scared of dogs, they can smell fear and you won't escape. I had a sense I wasn't going to be let off the hook from speaking to this woman who obviously wanted to exert some sort of superiority to the line. I had no idea who she was, she could have been the bloody Queen of Sheba for all I knew, I just didn't want to make small talk. Less than two minutes later she had finished the conversation with the lady in front of her and turned to me. 'And what are you being honoured for?' she said, casting half an eye over my white jacket. I don't really do glam, I am happier in gym gear, but there is a dress code when you meet royalty and you know me, I'm no rebel! I stood silent for a second or two and then just looked her in the eye like I was squaring up to an opponent in the ring. 'Boxing,' I said. And she just looked at me for a few seconds before she realised I wasn't joking, and just went, 'Oh!' And then that was it. She turned back around in the queue and didn't say a word to me.

There was no getting away from the nervousness I was feeling, it was so intense. While we were waiting patiently a very official-looking man explained to us what was going to happen and exactly what we had to do. It was a very slick operation and no one was allowed to go off-script or throw a spanner in this very regal, very traditional, well-oiled machine.

'When your name is called you walk forwards, curtsey, walk forwards again, curtsey again and then your first words are, "Your Majesty,"' said the official. 'You have about a minute and a half with His Majesty and then you leave, walking backwards so you don't turn your back on the prince.'

'Did we all get that?' he asked. There was a general hum of agreement, 'Yeah, yeah, yeah,' I thought, 'Got it.' And then the queue was formed. Well if I didn't forget everything I had just been told. I forgot everything the official-looking, guard-type servant man said as I watched people in front of me leave the line and walk forward when their name was spoken. Everything I had just been told had gone right out of my brain as I was just standing there and breathing in the air of my royal surroundings. And then, as the queue moved forwards I became even more nervous as I saw more of what was going on and more of the grand hall I was about to be walking into. And by this time my brain was all over the place and I tried to calm myself down. And then I started to think, shall I tell him I had lunch with Princess Di all those years ago? But then I decided that as we didn't get much time together then no, probably not. There were just a couple of people, including Harrods lady, in front of me now but by the time I started to realise that I needed to calm myself down I heard my name being announced!

'Jane Couch, services to boxing,' was the call.

'Shit!' I am thinking in my head and I start to strut up to the stage like some sort of tomboy gangster (that is how I am told I walk, it's not an conscious effort on my part, it's just something I seem to do!), messed up my first curtsey by doing some sort of weird half-bow-half-curtsey move and then moved forward again, forgot to curtsey and simply said, 'Alright mate!'

Well, when I think about it now I just cringe. All the protocol that I'd been told to adhere to only a short time ago and it all went out the bloody window. But it did make Prince Charles giggle. He really did. Who knows what he must have thought of me, but you know what, he absolutely didn't care one little bit and he put me at ease right away. I had totally messed up one of the most important moments of my life and not only did he laugh about it with me but he started a conversation right away to break the ice and smooth over my faux pas, asking me about boxing and whether I saw the recent Ricky Hatton fight in Las Vegas! I'm not convinced he watched the fight himself but he did know his boxing, he really did, and I thought it was such a cool thing for him to do, to immediately talk to me about Ricky and calm my nerves. And you know what else he said?

He said, 'I've got to say ...'

'What?' I replied.

'You're not as bashed up as I was expecting,' he said, with the biggest smile on his face.

'Yeah,' I said, 'I got away alright really ... but I used to be really good-looking!'

And he laughed. It was the best moment and we continued to chat about Ricky and boxing, and then a palace advisor came over to Prince Charles, saying, 'Sir, we have to move on,' and then that was it, time was up. I could have chatted away for hours with that man, he was so lovely. And fancy him telling me he was expecting me to be more bashed up! I'll never forget that, ever, it was just one of those moments I can instantly switch back to and it will put a smile on my face. And there weren't too many moments like that in my boxing career!

Afterwards, apart from posing for a few photos outside, it was time to go back to reality. There was no big celebration or anything with Mum, I had to go back to the farm and continue training as I had a fight coming up so I drove us both back to Bristol. Mum stayed in a local hotel that night and then I took her to the train station the next morning and she went back home. I was back on my own again, back in my nightmare.

Why did I stay at the farm and work my arse off while getting treated like shit for all those years? I don't have an answer, I just don't know. I was at the height of my fame in America and everyone thought I was doing alright, everyone thought I was living the life of Riley and I pretended I was. But I had no money, I had hardly any food, and I was living on a farm in the middle of nowhere. I had no friends and no family close by. Once the gym door was shut for the night, there was no one around. And Tex would say, 'It's OK, you can eat with us,' and yes, OK, that was a generous offer, but he just didn't get it. 'I don't want to eat with you!' I'd be screaming in my head. 'You're 70, your wife is in her 80s, I don't want to be here!'

But I was there. I spent many a night in my room on the farm on my own, in bed at 8 o'clock in the evening, feeling like I had nothing left in me anymore. My heart was breaking. I didn't know what I should do, I didn't know whether to continue to fight or just forget everything. It seemed like such a big effort, making decisions, and I didn't have the energy. I had all these world title belts but yet I had nothing. Here I was, training and training and training until I had nothing left to then fight in matches that would either be last minute, unpaid or unfairly scored. And many people don't realise the training involved to be a world-class fighter. It sounds unbelievable even now but it really is the most tedious, back-breaking, tough workout in the world and there can be weeks and weeks and weeks of it. And you get to a point when you think is this all fucking worth it? Is any of this worth my energy anymore? All my mates were going out and getting married and starting families and having fun, and look at me, I'd think. Look at me, crying my eyes out, on my own every night, knowing I had another full day of the same tedious training ahead of me again.

The build-up to a fight is always so immense and then you get the moment in the ring, you get to fight and you get to see if that moment is all worth it or not. But then that moment's over, and you're going back to the farm the next day. You're only as good as your last fight, that is what they say, so you have this at the back of your mind all the time. I need to be better, quicker, punch harder, move faster, connect better … but then a little light flashes in your mind, a little light of doubt that gets brighter and brighter that seems to be illuminating your life. Why are you bothering? What's the point? Those were the words the lights were shining on.

I didn't tell anyone how I felt. I had chased this dream for so long, I had given up my life for so long that, fucking hell, if I told them how I really felt ... I don't think I wanted to even contemplate that idea. Disappointed, of course, that was a given, but disappointment that hides their real thoughts – that I was just a failure. I tried to speak to my old trainer Frank a couple of times but it was hard to express to him how low I felt and our chats became less and less frequent. The more disappointed I felt in myself, the more I thought people would see it in me but a hundred times worse. So then I added shame to the list of things I was feeling too.

I was still doing the odd interview with the press, 'day in the life' interviews that centred around my training, interviews to keep interest up, Tex would say. And I'm sure I just lied my way through so many of them, I just didn't care anymore. 'Did I get my knuckles insured?' No, of course I bloody didn't, I wasn't insured full stop, but for the magazine journalist, the answer would be 'Yeah, yeah, course they are insured'. It sounds better doesn't it? I said things I thought they wanted to hear.

'We are told boxers are superstitious, are you superstitious Jane? Do you have any lucky mascots?'

No I'm not superstitious, of course I'm not, but I am full of shit and that journalist thought they were getting a huge insight to my world when I told him I'd kiss a four-leaf clover before every fight and how I'd always lace up my right boot before my left boot. I was saying what they wanted to hear. I didn't care. Write what you want, I thought.

I was at the farm for my whole boxing career – from my first fight in Copenhagen to my very last one in France. When I think about those years, the best years of my life, from my mid-20s to retiring at 40 years old, I just feel an overwhelming sense of sadness and grief for a person who knew nothing else, who didn't experience the life that other people her age were experiencing and yet was just concentrating on being the best boxer she could be and trying to make a living and a name for herself. But what did I really do? I only really succeeded in upsetting everyone, winning fights but not getting paid, accepting last-minute fights and getting pummelled … it's not a great legacy is it really? The last few fights I took part in? I couldn't honestly say what happened. I probably shouldn't have even boxed those last five or six, I didn't have it in me. I lost the last three, I know that much. It wasn't like I went out in a blaze of glory!

I was putting on a brave face to everyone. Mum came down a couple of times and when she did I knew she'd be thinking, 'This is a bit basic, a bit cold … but it must be what Jane wants so I won't say anything,' and I'd be thinking, 'This is hell Mum, get me out of here,' but I wouldn't say anything either. I didn't want to break the illusion that I was happy. This was my dream remember, my dream to be able to fight, and I was a boxer and I loved it. I could tell myself that a couple of times, and sometimes I believed it myself because I think at first it was easy to pretend. And if there were bad days, well, there would be bad days, but I could talk myself around. I'm still a bit like that now, if something goes wrong, 'Oh well, it's happened, cheer up, it will be OK tomorrow.' But it gets to a point when you can't talk yourself around anymore.

Mum was no fool either, she knew the sacrifices I was making to continue to box. The fact that I went out and chopped wood for the fire for my little wood burner, the fact that I kept chickens just so I knew I had eggs to eat, it sounds a bit like something from the 50s doesn't it?! And mums ... they are very aware of the little things. The little sparks that go from a person's eyes. I was the best bullshitter at pretending things were OK but I have no doubt Mum knew. I spoke to her a few years ago about it all and she told me that it wouldn't have done any good even if she had said to me to leave the farm, I wouldn't have listened to anyone. And she's right, I had to reach that point myself. However hard it got, it was something I had to do.

There were a few nice people who made all the difference in my life at the farm. Stu McKenzie, the biggest boxing fan you're ever likely to meet and one of the nicest humans in this business. He was such a support to me and became a really good friend. I am not sure where I would have been without him. And there was a girl called Midget, she was brilliant to have around the farm, and although she wanted to train as a boxer, she didn't want to compete. She'd come to the gym and spar but she wasn't interested in taking it any further. That was fine, there was no pressure and from my point of view it was just great to have another female around! And then there was Meg, a young girl who must have only been about nine years old when I first met her. She kept horses on the farm so would be up twice a day letting them out, mucking them out and then putting them to bed. I saw her so often it wasn't long before we started chatting and she'd be interested in what I'd been doing and asking me who I'd been fighting. She loved to hear my stories and we'd chat for ages. She was like a daughter I never had and over the years she did start calling me mother! She lived with her mum about 15 minutes away from the farm, and it was her mum who would bring me food – homemade meals to keep me going. I used to do without half the time. I used to pretend I had eaten, so she stopped asking me if I had and just brought me food, as she knew otherwise when I'd just say I was alright. And if I had to get weight off for an upcoming weigh-in, then I would try to justify not eating for a good reason. But the times I was really hungry, well, Meg's mum saved me.

Meg was only young then, she wasn't quite aware of what was going on but she said to me recently that she was pleased I was finally speaking about something I had bottled up for so long. She was proud of me, she said. I think you should meet her, reader, this is my Meg:

I met Jane when she lived on a farm as that is where my horses were kept. I was down there a lot, every day, twice a day with the horses. I was there for about eight or nine years and when I was about 11 or 12 years old I wanted to be a boxer too so started training in the gym. Because Jane lived there and trained there she was always around so it was very easy to get chatting and we've never really stopped since! From the outside, the farm probably looked quite impressive, glamorous even I suppose. So it's hard for people to hear that this beautiful place, this farm, that looks like the stuff of dreams, Jane called her prison. To the casual observer she had it all, she's living on a huge farm, has a gym to hand and can go training whenever she likes. But people don't see the other side of it.

When she left home to live on the farm she was in her mid-20s and suddenly she was with a bunch of strangers and she'd stay there for nearly 20 years. She became almost like a slave in a way, not that she was locked up physically or anything but her mind was captive. She had been drilled from such a young age. She set herself a goal, to be world champion, but there was no reward in a sense when she became one. It was just briefly acknowledged and then it was time to carry on again. My mum was feeding her meals, trying to keep her strength up with home-cooked food and Jane did admit to me, years later, that if it wasn't for my mum, she would have starved.

I have only eaten a banana today, she'd say to Mum. And sometimes she had to because of her training, she had to keep herself a certain weight to box, but other times she just didn't have a choice. Mum was running her own business at the time and she'd make a bulk load of food. When she'd pick me up from the stables we'd all pop into Jane's and she'd have a cup of tea waiting for us. Mum would always bring her down extra meals because she knew she wouldn't have anything and it just seemed normal to me in a sense. I was young at the time, I didn't realise she was struggling, I just saw my mum being mum and doing mum stuff like cooking for people! That's childhood innocence for you, but I had such a perceptive mum, she knew what was going on. And Jane never asked for anything, she never once asked for food or the meals Mum brought in. She wasn't one to say she needed help but Mum knew what was going on and this was her way of helping out. The problem was Jane had no one else. There was never a life outside anymore. She didn't go home very often, she was on the farm, living and training and that was it. There was no social life and the only interaction she had was with the people who came on to the farm or used the gym.

And for all her achievements she had nothing to show for it other than her belts. You see other people living lavish lifestyles at her level in the sport but she didn't have that. She had nothing. But she was blind to it, everyone was, we didn't realise in that world what was happening, it just was what it was. It's like the saying, when you're in the forest you don't realise how far you're in it until you come out! You don't realise, until you are out of that situation, how bad things were and then you get angry with yourself for not seeing it. Why didn't I do this? Why didn't I do that? But Jane didn't know any different. She was there from such a young age and when you've moved away from your whole entire family to the other side of the country, you know no different. Jane just concentrated on the fact that this was a job and she had to get on and do it. The farm was a routine, a way of life. Once everyone had gone home and that was it, it was just her left. There was no active life once the gym shut, just a few animals. There were no neighbours, it was just Tex and his wife and Jane. The gym and the livery yard made it busy during the day but the nights were long when it's just you left by yourself. And it was the same day in, day out, each day a repetition of the one before. For years, the same day over and over again and that was her life, until she left. She thought she was going to be there forever I think, and she didn't know anything else, everything in her life was all to do with training, all to do with boxing. That is all she has ever known. And now, she's out of it and I know she misses it but she's looking at it like a bad memory. There were good memories as well, she became five-times world champion for goodness sake, not many people can say that! And I do say to her all the time, 'Look at what you've done Jane, look how far you've come, you have made a mark on the sport!' But she doesn't look at it like that, she's oblivious to the fact she has done so much.

But there were times when she wasn't eating, she couldn't afford to, and she'd be driving around in these complete banger cars and I remember thinking, as a kid, why can't you have a flash car Jane?! For a world champion you expect something to show for it! I think people think she should be rich, have it all, lead a glamourous and successful life. When she decided, politely, to say 'fuck this,' it's probably the best thing she has ever done.

When she left, the farm went downhill. Without the pull of Jane Couch, it was just another training gym and it lost its appeal, it was getting tired. All the boxers slowly left afterwards and it eventually closed down completely. It has been shut for a couple of years now. If you're not getting boxers into the gym, not getting anyone in to train, you're not getting any income. They had to shut it down. Jane put the place on the map, when she left it was like she took the only bit of spark of it with her.

And the boxers who came to the gym in the first place were all there because of Jane essentially, people want to come and train and want her approval. People still recognise her all the time and ask her for pictures and she's still a person who people recognise but she doesn't know how to take it. She's such a novel person, she doesn't think she is anything special at all and yet she was such an inspiration to me! I had a few issues at school and she said to me, 'Come and do a bit of training with me' and never in a million years did I think that I'd ever become a fighter or anything like that. She put me straight in the ring in that first training session and I have fought ever since then. I was ten years old when I started with her and I'm 24 now and I've gone into MMA (Mixed Martial Arts) and cage fighting and we were doing a lot together and doing stuff with Ricky Hatton and meeting some great people. Now I look back and I think of all the stuff we did together. For boxers and martial arts women and men, she is a massive icon. It's only when I take a step back and realise she's not just a friend, she's an inspiration. To have someone like Jane close to me and yet so high up in the sport that I love, how many people can say they've got someone like that for a mentor? I can just send her a message, a five times World champion for goodness sake, and she'll come and help me. Who else can really say that? It would be like me texting Mike Tyson or Ricky Hatton! And we are such good friends, I can see how lucky I am. Some of the boxers around the world would give an arm and a leg for that sort of opportunity! I was training with her and she was helping me as much as she could, even though I knew her heart wasn't in boxing anymore. I could see it towards the end. I was older and I know she was less involved in the gym and less involved in training. She needed to be with people outside of boxing. She needed to break away from the farm and it was going to have to get worse before it got better. She did start to go out a bit more then, she didn't really care. She started doing some boxing promotions and would end up losing money to put on these shows. But she couldn't not care and she did it because she wanted to do the best for the boxers she was promoting. Again, everything was

around boxing, the promotions or the social events,
all connected to boxing. That was her life.

I asked Meg to contribute because she knew me so well at
the farm and I still find my time there hard to talk about. I
was living a robotic existence, I did for years, and it's hard to
differentiate one day from another. I was simply surviving
at the farm, but now I am living.

Before I completely gave up boxing I was asked to join
the BBBC. When I was fighting I had started to do a bit
of promoting – mostly myself as I didn't really have anyone
else doing it! – and then when I retired from fighting
completely I started promoting properly. That's when the
board invited me to join them and sit on the western area
council. I would be part of the group that would decide on
giving boxers a licence. They were giving me that power.
And it was so weird at first, I couldn't get my head around
why they had invited me to do that, only that I think I had
proven myself in a way. I had got the belts, I had got the
MBE, it looked good for them having me on the board I
guess. So I did join. I joined the panel that would decide
your fate. If you came in for a meeting and you'd applied
for a boxing licence, I would be one of the people sitting
watching you in the room and asking you, 'Why do you
want to box?' I was one of them now, one of the people who
had told me to fuck off all those years ago! And I can tell
you now, I didn't last long on the panel.

Do you want to know why I joined the board? I think I was optimistic that things had changed, I was hopeful that maybe, just maybe, things were different now, people were given chances, people who wanted to box were able to get a licence if they passed all the medicals and all the psychological checks. But I was deluded. Nothing had changed, it still felt like an unfair system of 'them' (the board) and 'us' (the boxers just wanting to make a living). I didn't feel proud of being part of that panel. Sometimes I would try and question what was happening but more often than not the response I got was, 'Shut up Jane.' That's all I got.

There were several active promoters on the board and if they had one of their fighters come in, they'd get a licence straight away. But if they had someone come in they didn't like they wouldn't give it to them. It brought back so many memories it was hard to deal with initially. I could picture myself there, in front of all these immovable, biased, sexist men ten years ago and I could see it clear as day, like it was yesterday, because that's how it felt.

I realised then it had been and probably always will be, a game. It's not whether you present yourself well or tick all the boxes, it's simply who you know. All these lads were coming up and sitting there and were so nervous because their future earnings, their livelihoods, depended on them getting a licence and it was all decided upon by a small group who seemed to like the power. I couldn't cope with it, I wasn't going to be part of it any longer, but for the time I was there I made sure I agreed every licence that was applied for, I never wanted to deny a boxer a licence, but after a while I just couldn't cope with the seemingly arbitrary decisions that were made.

It wasn't just boxers who'd be coming in for a licence, if you wanted to be a trainer or a promoter you needed a licence and we had approval for those too. These were even worse in a way and I felt that there were so many illogical decisions being made for reasons I just couldn't fathom. Applicants would be sent out of the room while the board made the decision and that's when the bitching began.

And some of the criticism was brutal, personal and, from what I could see, had no just reasoning or evidence to support a rejection of a licence. I was confrontational but I believed in fairness and I couldn't understand why all this criticism came out as soon as they left the room. I could argue against them all day long and with their decisions but it didn't get me anywhere. I couldn't unbend the bentness of this elite world.

I was on the board for about a year and probably the only reason I stuck it out for so long was because I had started to promote some lads and I wanted to give them every possible chance of succeeding. So if that meant keeping the board on side I would do it. I knew how difficult it was to get fights if the board and other promoters were against you. And it wasn't just about me anymore, I had a couple of boys who deserved my focus and for me to promote them the best way I could. I knew what it meant to them, what it had meant to me, and I didn't want to let anyone down. And I was done with fighting myself now, what else could I do? What else did I know? It was only boxing. But promoting turned out to be just as bad an experience as the fighting itself and I just thought, you know what, it is time to walk away. So I left the board and it wasn't a hard decision to make.

From this point on, I couldn't talk myself around anymore. There wasn't anything I could say to myself to justify it, to make things right. I couldn't convince myself that this boxing world was worth anything anymore. I just thought to myself, 'Fuck this shit'. I had retired from fighting but I was ready to retire from the whole boxing existence – fighter, promoter, manager … I was done.

Each morning I would wake up and just want the ground to swallow me up. I wanted everyone to forget who I was. I wanted to be a nobody, someone who wasn't expected to do anything or be anything, just anyone other than Jane Couch. I didn't want to be her anymore. And when you want to distance yourself from yourself, you just hit a brick wall and it wasn't long after that I had my breakdown. There was a constant noise in my head and instead of being physically punched, I felt like I was getting completely battered in my head, by my thoughts, my worries and my fears. What were Sara and Dinah going to think of me? How disappointed were they going to be in me, that they'd fought this massive, historic court case and now I was just throwing it all away? How pathetic will they think I am? How can I live with the thought that I'd let them down?

I was so down on myself, it was hard to see a way out. 'Why the fuck am I bothering with this anymore, what am I proving? I'm killing myself in the gym, why am I bothering?' I'd be thinking, every single day. And still, even at this time I was being asked to comment on women's boxing, why was it a good thing? I was asked over and over 'Why do I want to box?' by journalists, radio presenters and TV hosts ... and I began to realise I had no answer. I was a five-times world champion, I got my MBE and yet no one could get past the fact I was a woman and I was a boxer. And in the end, I had one answer to the question, 'Why do I want to box?'

I don't anymore.

Chapter Ten

And now I'll do what's best for me

'Until you're broken, you don't know what you're made of. It gives you the ability to build yourself all over again, but stronger than ever.'

Michael Fiore

CHOICE. That's what it boiled down to in the end. A choice. I made a choice to leave, leave boxing, leave fighting and leave a part of me behind at the farm.

I had nothing left. Years and years of sparring and fighting had caught up with me and it was time to stop. Did anyone try to persuade me to carry on? I wouldn't have listened to them if they did. But no one cared, not really. I just decided myself. Fuck the lot of them, I'm done. I retired at 40 years old, with five world title belts to my name, an MBE and what felt like the weight of the world on my shoulders.

Funnily enough, it was my big brother Tom who told me not to give up. 'Fuck everyone else Jane,' he said, 'just keep going, you'll be alright, just keep going.'

He always believed in me, he always supported me like I always believed in him. He was my childhood hero and in a sense he still is a hero of mine. He had a dream and followed it and is still bloody following it. He's not like the average man, he's still drumming now and he's 56 years old! I'm not a sheep, I don't follow anyone and I never have, and both Tom and I have done and decided to do our own thing. Nowadays, it seems things are so much more regimented for kids; they go to school, go to college, get a job, get married, have children … it doesn't suit every woman, why should it?

It definitely didn't suit me having kids, I was too busy to think about it when the time was right and it's no good looking back now and thinking 'what if'. Besides, it's not like I had a queue of boyfriends who wanted me to settle down and start a family, I probably scared off all potential suitors! Anyway, I think I would have been a useless mother. I'm not like my mum. I think about what she did for us growing up and how hard it must have been but the house was always full of love. We were a poor family but Tom and I didn't have a 'poor' upbringing in that sense. Being raised well doesn't mean we didn't drink or get into fights or smoke or use swear words. Being raised well was learning how to treat people – about manners and respect and accepting each other for who they are and what they wanted to do. We applauded Tom for leaving Fleetwood at 15 years old to follow his dream. Mum, who would have given everything she had in the whole world for me not to box, never once told me not to follow my dream. 'You can lie down for people to walk all over you and they will still complain that you're not flat enough.' I can't remember for the life of me who told me that but it's so true. I get it now. You're never going to please everyone, no matter how much you try to bend over backwards for them, it's better to just crack on with your life. No one else is going to live your life but you, so you just have to make the best of it.

And Tom and I did that when we were kids and we're doing it now. We learnt how to make a coal fire with nothing, we learnt survival, we learnt what was important, we had to. We were streetwise and we did stuff for ourselves and by ourselves, and we looked after ourselves. It's a good job we did just get on with it. It taught me how to get on with everything else I faced; I got on with fighting and training and fighting and training and I didn't curl up into a ball and swallow a load of pills and start self-medicating. Would anyone have blamed me? Probably not. But then I would have always lived with the idea of stuff I 'might' have done.

I might have been world champion. I might have changed the law. I could have done this or that ... no 'could have' here, I bloody did it and I bloody know how hard it was to do it. But I did.

So I had to start supporting myself again. I left the farm and decided to get myself a little flat, and it was during that time that the darkness took over and each day was an effort.

I let the pain, the bitterness, the unfairness and the sourness of what had been my experience of boxing envelop me until I couldn't see a way out or a future and I ended up going to hospital that day with my good friend Kim. She had been someone I had known at the farm and she helped save me.

Having a funeral, burying my boxing career on that warm sunny afternoon was just the beginning of a road to recovery, it was a start, a new direction. It didn't solve all my issues in an instant but it did help me put a lid on a chapter of my life that had turned sour. And even though that chapter was a large part of my life, I still had a lot of living left to do.

And, of course, it was hard. I didn't know anything else other than boxing and I didn't know anyone else, but I did it, I started again. Don't ever think you can't, at any age, say to yourself, right that's it, I'm done, time for a new start because if I can you can. I was 41 years old and I had to start thinking about making a new living and earning money again. I had tried being a manager after I quit fighting and did a bit of promoting and managing, but then I turned into the person who was saying the same things that I had been told in the past and that was just a massive wake-up call. I didn't feel comfortable being a manager and having a lad's career in my hands, I didn't feel like I could ever do a good enough job – not because I didn't care but because I knew the world that I was inviting this boxer to be part of didn't bloody care! I had to be the one to explain that you don't just get a fight that is put straight on TV, it's a case of working at it and taking every fight you can get, and then when you do get a fight you have to get up and go around all the pubs and all the clubs and all your friends and beg them to buy tickets because if you don't sell tickets, you don't fight, it's as simple as that.

'In order for you to fight,' I'd tell them, 'you have to sell a few hundred tickets to pay for that fight.'

I promoted a few shows with Ricky Hatton in the early days, when he first started promoting, and we both had the same focus with work – we were going to be there for the fighters. We had a few boxers with us and we put them on a show in Bristol and then the next thing you know they've gone to a big promoter because Ricky didn't have a TV deal for them and a big promoter did. Ricky was spending all his own cash promoting and there is so much work that goes into a show, it takes weeks and weeks getting it sorted, getting the opponents, ordering the ring, getting the venue, the hotels, and at the end of it, I'm not sure either of us made any money. But our lad got a win and that meant it was a good night for him, Ricky and me. But it's not just a one-off. You've got to keep constantly doing the shows and keep your boxer in the forefront of everyone's minds and there is so much time and effort and money involved.

And it will never change. Every boxer has to start somewhere, you all have to take those first hits – physically and mentally. I started in Fleetwood and had to go to Bristol, I had no choice, there was nowhere else, but if there had been, maybe if there were other options for me, I would have jumped ship, who knows? But you are still a small fish in a big pond and the system was just so stacked up against the lads I was dealing with and I wasn't going to hide the truth from them that it was bloody hard work and that they probably wouldn't ever make it big and that they would have injuries and scars and cuts and bruises and, quite honestly, not much else to show for it. I couldn't tell them any different. But you can't stop someone with a passion to box so if they sold the tickets then great, of course I'd be in their corner and backing them every step. The small promoters would be the ones bringing them through, getting them trained up, getting them through the fights and then all of a sudden you start to see you have a good fighter, you've brought them through 15 matches with 15 wins and no losses and it's then the sharks would circle again. The big promoters would take interest, would start to watch where your boxer was going, what they were doing, and if they liked what they saw, that was it. The lad you'd brought this far gets stolen from you with the offer of fame and money.

'Come with me now and we'll get you a British title fight on Sky,' they'd say. And you can't blame the boxers because, well, wow! It doesn't happen to a lot of them and now they are being offered fame and fortune, and even if it only lasts for a short while, they'll be boxing on TV and that dream will come true. But then what?

And meanwhile the promoter who has done all the hard work to begin with, to get the lad to a level that is now worthy of a big promoter, what happens to them? I used to speak to a lot of other promoters about this: 'How the hell do you do it?' I'd ask. It seemed to me that you're forgotten about as soon as you start to think your boxer could really get somewhere and then, all of a sudden, the big promoters come out from the woodwork with offers that your boxer can't refuse and then what?

Mickey Duff, the legendary boxing manager who had a short but furious boxing career before he decided to make a living on the other side of the ropes, said it best: 'If you want loyalty, buy a dog.' He was 100 per cent right and that is one of the most enduring truths there is when it comes to the boxing business.

And you can't blame a boxer for having their head turned ... I'd be getting them £600 or £700 a fight in the very early days and then as they started to get into the rankings and get offered title fights the sharks would say, 'You have to come with us now, we'll be able to get you the title fights now, we'll get you on TV.' It's not a hard decision is it?

So any time you see a boxer on TV, remember you didn't see their struggle to get there, the endless smaller fights and hard work that had gone on before. It's such a unique world, boxing, that generally people only get to see that one small part of it. The showy, flash, big-money bouts on TV. The before and after bits, the hard work and then the kicking to the kerb when you've served your purpose, no one needs to see that, do they?

And then throw in the promotional work too, the photo opportunities, the sponsors and the interviews.

Tex was always on at me to do more glamorous photoshoots, it was where the big money was he'd say, and I'd be livid when he even brought the subject up.

'Are you fucking mental, Tex?! I have just fought for so long to get the respect and recognition in women's boxing and all you want me to do is get my tits out?!'

It was just crap. And it didn't matter what press I did, they didn't ever pay off! I didn't see hardly any money for all that time I spent doing it – all the time I could have been training or boxing and earning money.

And yet, I was, at the time of my court case, one of the most famous boxers in the country. When they did a reader poll in *Boxing Monthly* magazine, the three most famous boxers in the entire United Kingdom were, according to the voters, Prince Naseem Hamed, Lennox Lewis and me. I was in third place. And not for any of my boxing accomplishments, because of the court case!

And, again, I'd be thinking, 'OK, that's great, but what about my fights?' I fought good people, I had cracking fights, I was quite often fight of the night in America, where my bouts were shown to millions of people on the huge TV networks like ABC, what about all that?

What about the world titles I had won? And it didn't matter how frustrated I got about it at the time, I realise now, you can't change the way people remember you or recognise you or what image they have of you. I probably will, for a lot of people, just be remembered for being the supposedly 'crazy' lady who hit Michael Barrymore on TV, or for winning some sort of court case, although they won't remember the exact details, but never for boxing with some of the biggest names in the world, on the same card as them and blowing their matches out of the water because my fights were always the most entertaining and most spectacular fights of the night.

Does that hurt me? Does that thought make me angry? I can, hand on my heart, tell you no. Not anymore. There is just no feeling there anymore. After my breakdown, my relationship with boxing was non-existent. There was no relationship anymore, I was done. I took an interest in that I followed who was fighting. I would see names come up in the newspaper and read their stories, but it's a very one-sided relationship. Boxing has no hold on me and I can take it or leave it as I see fit. Meg reckons I still get itchy fingers if I ever see a boxing bag now. Ha! Maybe. I could go to a boxing match and I could sit and watch it and I just know, I know everything that goes on. I look at it with different eyes now, all-seeing eyes, because I know what it's like. I've seen the way that you have to get a licence, I've seen the way people are treated and the way the big promoters and managers play god with people's lives behind the scenes. I've seen the way managers pretend to care about their boxers. I've been in dressing rooms with boxers before a fight and I have seen the people all crowding round them, making noise, pumping them up, getting them going. And I have seen the same fighters sitting alone in their dressing rooms when they have lost their fight. All alone, in the quiet. No one was with them then. Nobody cared then.

I saw a lot of desperate boxers trying to make it big to no avail. For a few years after I stopped fighting and promoting, a friend of mine, Rita, and I decided to start up our own YouTube channel. We'd go around interviewing all sorts of people – boxers, promoters, trainers – to then post on YouTube. It was, at the time, great fun. I'd meet lots of new people, promote fights on YouTube, so in my own way I'd help a little and people would know me and more often than not be happy to chat and tell me about their fights and their training. And I suppose there was still a part of me that wanted to hang on by a thread to this world, who still wanted to have some sort of affiliation with it.

And it was fun for a while, the parties after the shows especially. I think I made up for years of being good and training and not partying when all my mates were! But Rita and I would be travelling around the country to keep getting new videos so it quickly became expensive and it quickly lost its appeal when you saw more and more of the behind-the-scenes shit that went on. You are dealing with people's lives and yet the mantra for most of the promoters and managers was simply are they serving a purpose? And if not, time to move on. There are one or two managers out there and one or two promoters who are good, decent people who wouldn't use and abuse a fighter but it's a very, very small percentage of boxers who make it, who get to the top, who are any good.

So even when I try to be indifferent to boxing now, to try to see it like a fan on TV, I can't because I can't unsee or unlearn everything that I know to be the truth.

I've learnt to let go and it was the best thing I ever learnt. Letting go was painful, change was painful but nowhere near as painful as staying stuck somewhere I didn't belong. I guess sometimes it's good to just say I'm done. I'm not angry or upset anymore, just done. I've learnt what it is to be a strong person, I always knew I had to be physically strong, but this mental game, this mental strength, I have learnt how to get that. I know a strong person isn't a person who doesn't cry or show emotion. A strong person is someone who does all of that and then gets up to fight again. And I think until you are broken or have been hurt or been at the lowest point you will ever be, you don't know what you are made of. You don't know your inner strength. And now I have the ability to build myself up all over again. I know it was easier for the Frank Maloneys of the world to make me out to be a bad, horrible person because then they didn't feel guilty when they slated me. And I would say to him, or anybody that says, 'Oh, you shouldn't let the bad stories get to you,' or 'Don't worry about what is written, ignore the criticism,' that's all well and good but that endless criticism and endless negativity and endless attack from the media leaves its mark. You can't ignore it. You don't get used to it and it always hurts. But probably my life's greatest lesson was learnt at the worst time – I had a breakdown but it was also my breakthrough.

And my life now? I love my life so much now, it's amazing. And it's true what they say – when people are at the lowest points in their lives they discover, in the blink of an eye, that the most amazing moments in life are still a possibility, that there is light at the end of the tunnel! I was dealing with the aftermath of my breakdown when I met a man called Brian and I have never looked back.

I met him at a hotel by the airport. It was a bit of a random place but I had been doing an interview for a friend of mine with a magazine about Bristol and something had gone wrong and it basically meant we had to redo everything the following day. We found a convenient little hotel by the airport to stay in so we'd be ready to start again but it just so happened that a man called Brian was also staying in that hotel. He is a HGV driver and he was flying back to Ireland the following day after completing a job. So if you believe in fate, it was fate. I should have been at home that night but instead I was staying in a hotel next to an airport and started chatting to the man who was to change my life.

'I'm going back to Ireland tomorrow,' he said.

'Never mind,' I said. I didn't want to seem too keen!

'Can I have your phone number?'

And that was that. I gave him my mobile number and then the next day I got a text from him saying, 'If I find you in Bristol will you go on a date with me?'

That made me laugh. He had to find me first, that would be a challenge I thought. But he bloody did, although I reckon he cheated because when he next landed at Bristol airport he asked a taxi driver to find me, which of course was easy for a cabbie, they know everyone and everything that happens, they are the fount of all knowledge! And then that was it. He moved in with me, there was no real conversation about it, and he's been here ever since! I was living in an old market part of the city by then and I was making a conscious effort to go out and socialise. I wanted to be out and near people, I wanted the company. I had spent too long feeling lonely and being isolated on the farm, I wanted to feel alive again.

So after my breakdown and the funeral I set myself challenges. I'd go into town every day, I'd speak to strangers, I'd spend time with homeless people, I'd try to help them if I could and nowadays it is a big passion of mine, I will be making sure I can, in any way I can, help those who need it. I've found relatives for some of these guys who have spent too many years of their lives thinking that no one cares about them. I managed to track down some long-lost children for a homeless man who became a big part of my life and I have never been more proud of the moment that they met shortly before he died. Everything gets put into perspective then, of course it does, there is no time to feel sorry for yourself, you are dealing with life and death, with family, with love. And being out of the farm, being out with people again, I felt alive. My life was slowly getting back on track and I was still taking medication but I felt a lot more in control. So when Brian came into my life, I finally understood what was important in life, and it wasn't boxing! And being loyal to the wrong sort of people ... another lesson learnt. Being loyal to the right people is a lot more rewarding. It just took me a lot longer to catch on to this idea than most people, I suppose. But I got there in the end. I know I am a decent person, I know I have a good heart at the end of the day and I know that means good things will eventually come my way. So when I retired, all the bad things that I had been through ... well, everything just came good. See, I guess I am a decent person!

And the best thing about meeting Brian? He had absolutely no idea who I was, not a clue. I suppose he probably thought the taxi driver knew me personally when he first found me until he began to understand that I was fairly well known in Bristol because I was Jane Couch 'the boxer'. It was brilliant that he didn't know who I was, it put us both on an equal, level playing field and I knew his interest in me was genuine – not built on reputation or stardom or anything I had done before. I knew the perils of this business, I had learnt that people might seem to take a genuine interest in you but they are only really interested because you are famous and they think they might be able to get something out of the relationship. And it's flattering, of course it is, I know how it feels when you have hundreds of people watching you fight and cheering and clapping you. You believe that every single one of those people think you're great and want to be your friend. I've seen boxers, the really famous ones, with the crowds of people all around them, all wanting a piece of them, telling them they're the best, the bees knees, the champion. And in that bubble, they believe it, they live off it, they get used to it and boxing teaches them to accept it and relish it. And boxing teaches them that hundreds of thousands of people will be watching them box and watching their shows and cheering for them. So when they step out of that bubble, out of that environment, that's it. You are just you again. It's so false and so cruel and yet you see it happening constantly and it will continue to happen.

The only reason anyone knows who I am really is because I was doing all of those TV interviews and radio shows and all I was doing was letting them take the piss out of me. My fame came from boxing but not because I was winning fights. And yet in America I was regarded as a boxer. I had boxed in one of the biggest shows in the world, with the biggest TV audience of millions, and I was seen as a boxer rather than as someone who knocked out Barrymore, or someone who always got into an argument about why women should be allowed to box in this country. It's like, if you're a famous singer you'll probably only really be known for one song, or the way a football player is only really known for the bad incidents. I know there was a time in my life when I thought I should just go around trying to knock out all the TV presenters I could find and be done with it. If you can't beat 'em join 'em eh?

But then I had the likes of Dinah and Sara at the back of my mind, people who I admire and who cared about me. They didn't take anything from me, they just helped me and they understood the sacrifices. They understood what it meant to me and when we won the court case, I didn't want to be the one disappointing them by saying I wanted to quit. I just thought with all the hard work they had put into my case, all the effort they had put into me, to help me, they would be so disappointed. But I should have known, they didn't worry about boxing, they just wanted me to be alright.

I wish I had that outlook and that confidence – when you watch someone like Dinah in action, it's remarkable. She was just so brilliant and passionate about what she did. They both made such a big impression on me, Dinah and Sara, and even though they were only in my life for the court case, they cared. They didn't take from me, they gave me something. The impact they had on my life was phenomenal because they cared. They were so posh and so intelligent and yet they cared for someone like me! I would not have won that case if I had had anyone else. But I had Dinah and I had Sara and there was no way anyone was getting past them. It's quite often I read that if it wasn't for me another woman would have come along and they would have made history and they would have won the court case. But no one will ever do what I did because what I did, I did with no support, no backing, no money, no one on my side. Yes, the uproar would be huge now if women's boxing was illegal in this country right at this moment, there would be the most tremendous amount of support, the most tremendous hullabaloo if it went to court. The subject of equality is huge now, and rightly so. Back then, well, I felt like I was on my own. I do remember one man, Rod Robertson, who came to my trial. He was head of the ABA (now the Amateur Boxing Association of England, ABAE) at the time and a really decent, nice fella. I asked him why he was in court and he didn't mince his words. He told me he'd been sacked from the ABA because a couple of years ago he had recommended that women should be allowed to be amateur boxers. He'd read about my case and he wanted to see for himself the moment that women's boxing became legalised in this country.

He was a commander in the Royal Navy I think and he was in his 60s then, an older man with old-fashioned beliefs and yet he was so, so supportive. He had tried to let women into the amateur world two years before he saw me in court and he was there to make sure something he believed in, a person's right to box, no matter their gender, was upheld. And Rod was like us, he couldn't believe what he was hearing, the ridiculous case the BBBC had presented. He kept looking over at me and shaking his head and when I spoke to him afterwards he just seemed so deflated. 'It's not that bad Rod,' I said and he just looked at me sadly and replied, 'It is Jane, it's terrible.'

They had no defence, there never was a defence, they were just hoping everyone felt the same way as them. They didn't realise there is another world outside of boxing, it's not just them in their bubble, detached from real life. So when it was announced in August 2009 that women's boxing was going to be included as a sport in the London 2012 Olympics I was over the moon. It was a momentous day, a day that most people probably didn't think would ever come. The press of course wanted me to comment, to say my bit about it, and I was happy to. But then the old stories about me would be dished out again, the 'street fighter from Fleetwood who liked beating up a copper'. Yawn. It was getting stupid now, give me some credit, I'd think, try to be original!

My adjectives didn't detract from the historic news that women's boxing had been officially accepted in this country. And not just by this country, by the International Olympic Committee, who wanted to see the sport celebrated on one of the world's biggest sporting stages. It was a phenomenal achievement. And it was only going to get better. Not only would we get to see televised fights with female boxers from Great Britain, by including it in this acclaimed sporting arena we'd potentially get more and more girls watching it and wanting to take it up professionally. What a legacy that would be.

There were 286 boxing competitors taking part in the 2012 Olympic games and of those 36 were women. It was hardly a massive number but it was a start, for the first time at any Olympic games, women would be taking part in three boxing events and I was so proud of all of them. The BBC gave it great coverage and everything was so positive and encouraging. I remember exactly where I was when we watched Nicola Adams win her gold medal. I was in a bar in Bristol and it was just absolutely fantastic, a fantastic day for women and for women in the future. I cheered like the rest of the bar when the referee held her glove aloft in the air, declaring her the gold medal winner. And Katie Taylor, when she won gold for Ireland, I just had the biggest grin on my face; another brilliant fighter showing the world what she could do. I was pretty astounded when Nicola Adams mentioned my name in an interview after winning her gold medal. She had no need to say anything at all about the history of women's boxing and yet she did. And if there was ever a time that I truly thought I had done something, if my life had made any sort of difference, that was it. A stranger thanking me for being the person who allowed her to be where she was right at that moment. A gold medal winner in women's boxing.

I think what it all comes down to is what you've learnt. I've learnt that things don't always turn out the way you planned or the way you think they should. I've learnt that having a dream and believing in that dream is important but you have to recognise when that dream becomes a nightmare. And if you don't wake up from a nightmare, it will darken both your days and your nights. I've learnt that I can get through bad times and I can keep looking for better ones. I've learnt to accept that things are the way they are now, with women boxing in this country, with gold medals won in a sport that I made legal in this country, and that it was, in part, a little bit down to me. And I've learnt to finally be proud of that.

Epilogue

The legacy

*'A river cuts through rock, not because of its
power, because of its persistence.'*

Jim Watkins

WOULD you ever go back into that world of
boxing? I get asked this question a lot. No,
never again. I don't want or need to be in that
world ever again. I will keep abreast of what is happening,
I will follow boxing folks on Twitter and I will throw in
my tuppence-worth every now and again, but I couldn't
bring myself to enter that domain properly again. I know
Meg says I get itchy fingers when I am near a boxing bag
but I can't help that, that's like a conditioned response I
think now! And, of course, I'm always there for Meg, I'll
help her as much as she needs me to – with training, with

advice, with support. But she knows my heart isn't there anymore, she doesn't expect me to be anything more than I am to her now. And I'm bloody proud of her, that's for sure. She is a top girl. She doesn't drink, she doesn't smoke. She would spar with all the men when we were at the farm, she was part of the family and she is still a big part of our lives now. I bought her her first car! She's a sensible lass, however much she goads me when she's watching women boxing now, and will text me or call me and say, 'You'd kill these girls Jane, you'd beat them easy!'

Are you meant to have regrets in life? Are they helpful? I guess my biggest regret is that I didn't see what a degrading and soul-destroying place the boxing world was sooner. I'm 51 years old now, I retired ten years ago after being in boxing for over 15 years, and there is a part of me that wishes I had woken up sooner. But that sort of regret isn't helpful and I have dealt with all that now. Life goes on and having a funeral for my boxing career meant I could lay that past to rest.

I suppose I regret not having people like Dinah or Sara in my life sooner, but that can't really be classified as a regret as I wouldn't have met them if it wasn't for boxing. I think I meant that I wish I had met people like them when I was younger, people like Sara and Dinah, who are honest and supportive and well-grounded, amazing women – would my life have gone any differently if I had met them when I was a teenager? Imagine having someone like that in your life as a kid. People looking out for you who cared about you as a person and not just as a fighter. Proper managers that didn't just use you and dump you as soon as you became worthless. But if I hadn't lived through that, I wouldn't be here to tell the tale and I probably wouldn't be as streetwise as I am now. I don't see things through rose-tinted glasses or soften things up to make people feel better. I know that for every success story there are thousands of boxers who are homeless, or in jail, or struggling with addictions, or haven't got a pot to piss in or a window to throw it out of. And I'm talking about really good fighters who now, well, they've been discarded from the world. There are hundreds of fighters out there who you wouldn't have a clue about let alone the ones you do, like Ricky, who've been to hell and back.

I have met so many celebrities and famous people in my life, I think that's what kept me going you know.

When I got moments like that, with Princess Diana and Prince Charles, it made it worth it. Money couldn't buy that sort of experience, boxing gave me that opportunity. That day, that afternoon, it was then that I realised somebody like her, who could make an effort with someone like me and not get anything out of it, it made me think, actually we're not that far apart really. Yes, we're worlds apart, of course, but we think along the same lines if you boil it down to the fact that she cared. It's not about how much money you have in the bank or whether you live in a palace or a council estate, it's who you are, what you give to the world, that's what counts. I've met some amazing people and I've been to some of the most amazing places and if I hadn't gone through what I did, I wouldn't have met some of these people. If I hadn't decided to box, I wouldn't have met my first trainer Frank. If I hadn't decided to try to box in my own country, I wouldn't have met Dinah or Sara. If I hadn't continued to box, even with the press and the promoters and the world against me, I wouldn't have met Princess Diana or Ricky Hatton or Prince Charles or Meg or the many other boxers and champions and legends. And it's about those moments, the ones that make you stronger and the ones that make you appreciate what you've been through, and make you realise it is somehow worth it.

Even through all the doom and gloom, even through the darkness that many boxers will recognise, I've come out of it. I've survived. If I can do it, anyone can. Through all the bad things, there are good things. Even now, I could ring Ricky Hatton up and have a chat all night and if it wasn't for boxing I wouldn't be able to do that, would I? If it wasn't for boxing I wouldn't have Meg, who I think of as family, in my life. And then there's Brian. OK, I didn't meet him directly through boxing but he came into my life at the time I needed to find a connection with something else, with someone else. And ten years later, we are still going strong! I have the most wonderful time with Brian, I can't imagine my life without him.

So I guess what boxing took off me one way, it gave it back in another. I help who I can because of what I did and what I went through. I'll go out on to the streets and into shelters and help homeless people; boxing has given me the confidence to do that, to talk to people and show them that I have dealt with the darkness. It's made me who I am today. I saw my doctor in town the other day and I told her I was writing a book about my life and she was very chuffed.

'That'll do you the world of good Jane, well done,' she said. And she was right. I finally feel such a sense of release, of liberation, to be able to speak about my career as a boxer and have no concerns whatsoever.

In the boxing world, the higher up the ladder you go, it's still corrupt. It probably always will be. But I can say things now that I wasn't able to say when I was boxing about the ruthlessness because I don't care, it is what it is. I can say it and I will say it. And it needs to be said. And I'm not bitter towards anyone now, not one little bit, and that's important for me to get across because now I have no bones with them at all. I just take the piss out of them now. I will say to them exactly how it is.

I still read things in the papers every now and again and I still like to be vocal on Twitter when I see the unfairness of it all. Frank Maloney, only a few years ago, so I should probably call him Kellie, was still spouting off about women and boxing and still using my name to get his message across in his column. 'The interest [in women's boxing] is just not there and never has been going back to the days when Jane Couch was a pioneer female professional. She was always pressing me to promote her but I declined. On reflection I was probably risking a right-hander as the formidable "Fleetwood Assassin" once flattened a bloke in a Blackpool bar when he kept patting her bum after she asked him to stop!'

Oh Frank ... if only any of this still mattered! I probably should be flattered he still wants to talk about me I guess, bless him.

Although I like to think that I paved the way for female boxing, there are a number of good fighters out there who will keep that flame burning. Only a couple of years ago Nicola Adams and Katie Taylor were in the press arguing that there should be an extension for the boxing rounds to increase in length to three minutes, meaning there would be four three-minute rounds rather than four two-minute rounds each fight. 'Female boxing has come a long way since Jane Couch MBE made the sport possible here in the UK in 1998,' said Nicola. 'However, there is still a way to go until both male and female boxers can campaign under the same competition rules.'

And Nicola is right, women's boxing has come a long way since the court case. The good news is because I had it so hard, because I had so much crap thrown at me left, right and centre, no one else should ever have to face what

I did. And please God I hope no one ever will. But do I think women's boxing will ever be taken seriously? Do I think it will ever get the same respect and support that is afforded the men? No. Another 50 years maybe and they might be on the same level playing field, not in boxing, women in sport in general. I just don't ever think it will happen in boxing, which is why I say to anyone now, male or female boxers, just say it how it is. If you are treated like crap, say it, don't try to please them, you'll be dragged into something dark and depressing and you'll just be chewed and spat out. If you can be true to yourself and good to other people, well, that's all it needs, isn't it? What the boxing world needs, what the world needs.

So back to the 'do I regret it' question. I know lots of people who regret things they didn't do in life and I think that would have been a lot harder for me to deal with. I could have easily given up when I was told that girls weren't allowed to box when I went into that first gym back in Fleetwood. That could have been it, I could have given up and spent a lifetime regretting not seeing boxing through, wondering what might have been. There would have been no world title, no court case, no history made, no breakdown.

But you know what, in the end, I think we always regret the chances we didn't take more than the ones we did that didn't go to plan. And of course, calling the decisions I made mistakes or regrets is over-simplifying things, because if I chose to do something at the time, the decision was made. I never purposely chose to make mistakes, that's the benefit of hindsight.

Yes, the fight to get women boxing was terrible but look what we achieved. The girls now, who can just go into a gym, any gym, and not have any of the shit that I had, that's what it's all about. It's just ... well, brilliant isn't it?

Acknowledgements

TO all my friends that have been there for me over the years and are still here today, you know who you are, and I want to thank you for helping me through the dark times.

I truly believe that if Sara, Dinah and I had not taken the board to court in 1998, women's boxing would not be what it is in the UK today and I was then, and still am, proud to have been part of that historic achievement.

My advice to boxers will always be to not take anything too personally. The boxing world can be amazing but it can be equally heart-breaking. Always have a plan for your life after boxing because once you stop fighting, that's it. Get in and get out and hopefully you won't be too damaged – physically or mentally – in the process.

Try to stay in touch with the few genuine people you do meet along the way, live life to the full and, most of all, be proud you even stepped into the ring.

Also available at all good book stores

9781785313684

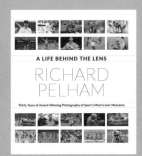

9781785315466

9781909626522

9781785313196

9781785313950

9781785314438

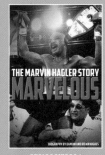

9781909178854

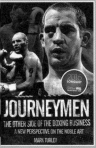

9781909626539

9781785312984

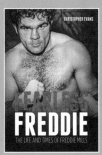

9781785312823

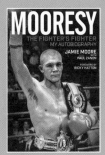

9781785311796